MATTHIAS PHILIPZEN

cajon

A BOX FULL OF RHYTHM

 Voggenreiter

Cover: OZ, Essen (Katrin & Christian Brackmann)
Layout: Notensatzstudio Nikolaus Veeser

Translated by: Sylkie Monoff

© 2008 Voggenreiter Publishers
Viktoriastr. 25, 53173 Bonn / Germany
www.voggenreiter.de
Phone: + (49) 228 / 93 575-0

ISBN: 978-3-8024-0677-5

Table Of Contents

STYLES

Table Of Contents – CD INDEX:

CD 2:

Track 1: CHAPTER 11:
           Cajinto Grooves - Bossa Nova
Track 2: CHAPTER 11: Cajinto Grooves - Samba
Track 3: CHAPTER 11: Cajinto Grooves - Baiao
Track 4: CHAPTER 11: Cajinto Grooves - Cascara
Track 5: CHAPTER 11: Cajinto Grooves - Swing
Track 6: CHAPTER 11: Cajinto Grooves - Hip Hop
Track 7: CHAPTER 11:
           Cajinto Grooves - Hip Hop (Variation)
Track 8: CHAPTER 11:
           Cajinto Grooves - New Orleans
Track 9: CHAPTER 11:
           Cajinto Grooves - Up Time Shuffle
Track 10: CHAPTER 11: Cajinto Grooves - Pop
Track 11: CHAPTER 11: Cajinto Grooves - Songo
Track 12: CHAPTER 11: Cajinto Grooves - Soca
Track 13: Styles: African Shuffle
Track 14: Styles: Alea Six
Track 15: **PLAYALONG: Full Version Style:**
           6/8-Title: Lost Memories
Track 16: **PLAYALONG: Clickversion Style:**
           6/8-Title: Lost Memories
Track 17: Styles: Blues
Track 18: Styles: Samba
Track 19: **PLAYALONG: Clickversion Style:**
           Samba Basic Title: Sobrado
Track 20: **PLAYALONG: Clickversion Style:**
           Samba Traditional Title: Carolina
Track 21: Styles: Partido Alto
Track 22: **PLAYALONG: Fullversion Style:**
           Partido Alto Title: Jatai
Track 23: **PLAYALONG: Clickversion Style:**
           Partido Alto-Title: Jatai
Track 24: Styles: Bossa Nova
Track 25: **PLAYALONG: Fullversion Style:**
           Bossa Nova Title: Caetano
Track 26: **PLAYALONG: Clickversion Style:**
           Bossa Nova Title: Caetano
Track 27: Styles: Hip Hop
Track 28: **PLAYALONG: Clickversion Style:**
           Hip Hop Title: This one is for you
Track 29: Styles. New Orleans
Track 30: **PLAYALONG: Full Version Style:**
           New Orleans Titel: Little Trawlers
Track 31: **PLAYALONG: Clickversion Style:**
           New Orleans Title: Little Trawlers
Track 32: Styles: Country

Track 33: **PLAYALONG: Clickversion Style:**
           Country Title: Jolly Jumper
Track 34: Styles: Rumba de Flamenca
Track 35: **PLAYALONG: Fullversion Style:**
           Rumba de Flamenca Title:
           St. Jean de Luz
Track 36: **PLAYALONG: Clickversion Style:**
           Rumba de Flamenca Title:
           St. Jean de Luz
Track 37: Styles: Martillo
Track 38: Styles: Compas
Track 39: Styles: Buleria
Track 40: Styles: Baiao
Track 41: **PLAYALONG: Fullversion Style:**
           Baiao Title: Amarante
Track 42: **PLAYALONG: Clickversion Style:**
           Baiao Title: Amarante
Track 43: Styles: Merengue
Track 44: Styles: Reggae
Track 45: **PLAYALONG: Style: Reggae Clickversion**
           Title: Liquid Groove
Track 46: **PLAYALONG: Style: Reggae Clickversion**
           Title: Sparkling Maracuja
Track 47: Styles: Soca
Track 48: **PLAYALONG: Fullversion Style:**
           Soca Title: Olhos Castanhos

PREFACE

The cajon is nothing more than a wooden box and that is why it has fascinated me since I first came across it stowed away on top of a shelf in a music store. At first no one could actually tell me what it was or how versatile its use is, let alone how to play it.

In recent years this has changed drastically. In the early 1970s, Flamenco music helped make the cajon become known in Europe. In the beginning, its musical existence was limited to being a mere "rumba box". But at the end of the 1990s it became an in demand percussive instrument for all kinds of musical styles.

The cajon was developed in Cuba and also in Peru in the middle of the 19th century. Slaves used it as a drum substitute after the government had forbidden them to play the drums and all their instruments had been confiscated.

I often use the cajon as a drum substitute. It's an ideal accompaniment for unplugged sessions, which means when you're just playing with non-amplified instruments.

This book is meant to help you learn more about the cajon and to inspire you to develop your own rhythms and sounds on this special instrument.

Construction And Maintenance Of The Cajon:

The cajon consists of three components: The striking surface or head, the body and a rattling or snaring device. If these three elements are adjusted well, it will allow for a perfect instrument.

The striking surface:

This is primarily made from plywood, which means it consists of several layers of wood and is therefore extremely solid although it is only a thin sheet. The kinds of wood that are applied most frequently are:

Beech: dry and very rich "bottom-end" sound, bright and clear tone on the edges.

Burlwood: warm, middle-register sound; my personal favorite.

Zebrawood: combines both sound characteristics: a rich bass tone and a warm, bright-sounding sound on the edges.

You will not be able to break the striking surface with your bare hand. If you use rods or brushes as described at the beginning of this book (p. 15), you can produce new and interesting sounds on the cajon.

Never use drum sticks on the instrument and remove any rings you may be wearing on your fingers!

The striking surface is screwed to the top section, which guarantees a high-pitched and tight sound when playing on the edge. If over the course of time the striking surface becomes slightly loose and starts moving away from the body, this is actually wanted and even deliberately forced by certain players by slightly loosening the outer screws on the left and right edges (never loosen the middle one). I never do this because the sound of the edges has enough volume when it is in the factory setting and the cajon develops a better sound the longer it is being played.

The pitch difference between the bass and edge sound, however, will remain. Therefore, you should like it already when you pick the instrument.

The body:

The body has a resonating hole on the back side (sometimes on the side) and consists of different kinds of woods depending on the wood of the striking surface. The regular size is 50 cm (20") and there are some with a sitting height of 45 cm (18") for the slightly shorter player. It is interesting how much impact the missing 5 cm (2") have on the sound, especially on the bass of the cajon. The bass of the smaller cajon has more pressure although it is of a higher pitch.

The rattling device:
The String Cajon "La Peru"

When lightly tapping on the striking surface, you can hear a metallic sound apart from the warm wooden one. The Peruvians experimented quite early with guitar strings that they attached at the back of the striking surface. This provided a sharper, more transparent sound and a clear distinction between the edge and the bass tone. Based on this idea, the German company Schlagwerk Percussion developed a tunable string system which covers the striking surface on the back with guitar strings stretched in a V-shape. This system has been beyond comparison to the present day and ensures a very sensitive response with rich overtones.

The Snare Cajon "Two in One"

This system is using the bottom of the small drum (wires which are attached under the reso-

nance head of the small drum), When cut in two parts, it was mounted on a saddle and jammed in a widget behind the striking surface. The advantage of this when compared to the string system is that the saddle may be removed with one pull of the hand. This way you'll receive another dry and warm wood sound without the metallic bite (Cuban sound). The disadvantage is that you cannot influence the relation between the wood and the snare sound. Besides, the sensitivity of the two-in-one instrument cannot be compared to the "La Peru" string model at all.

In the end, however, this is a question of personal taste. It is important which instrument sounds best to you under your hands!

Always keep your cajon well protected during transport; you can buy special bags and cases for this at music stores.

HOW TO MIC THE CAJON:

There is an endless number of ways to mic the cajon. I'll show you two ways how to do this, which have proven themselves for my sound expectations in the studio as well as on stage.

Preparing the instrument:

In order to muffle the overtones and amplify the bass, place a piece of foam in the cajon (on the bottom of the instrument!)

Live situation on stage:

I always use a small clip mic (AKG M 519) that is attached on the edge of the resonance hole in the back.

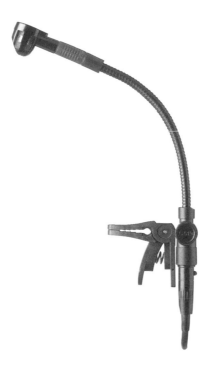

The advantage is that this makes me very flexible because it allows me to go to the edge of the stage for a solo part without having to worry about a mic stand. Play around with the gooseneck to which the mic head is attached. The further you bend the neck down, the more bottom the sound will have.

Studio Recording:

In order to record the instrument perfectly, I use two microphones. I place a bass drum mic (AKG D 112) approximately 5 cm (2") in front of the sound hole and another microphone (AKG Perception 150) in front of the striking surface for the high end and the soft strokes. The engineer now records the two mics on two different channels and will later be able to create the perfect sound from the mix of these two inputs.

CAJON COMPARSA

This cajon is roughly equivalent to the pitch of bongos. It is played between the knees as well. The two playing surfaces are tuned to a high and a low pitch, which provides the player with many sound variations.

Sound examples: **CD 1 Tr 1**

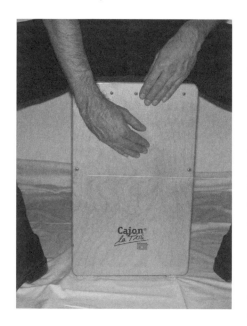

CAJON LA PERU

This is the most frequently used cajon which serves as the basis for this book. The player sits on the instrument and charms high-pitched, tight sounds out of the top edge and low deep ones when hitting the surface shortly above its center.

Additionally, the instrument is equipped with an adjustable stringing behind the striking surface. The strings provide an extra snare effect, which makes every stroke even more concise.

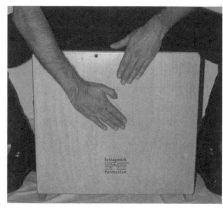

Sound examples: **CD 1 Tr 2**

BASSCAJON

As its name implies, this is the instrument with the lowest pitch! The player sits on the bass cajon producing high-pitched tones on the edge and a low bass sound in the center of the striking surface. Additionally, two strings are attached behind the striking surface, which produces a more concise sound.

For more than 25 years, the German Schlagwerk Percussion company has manufactured cajons which I think are the best on the market with respect both to their quality and sound. [www.schlagwerk.com]. I have listed the three cajon models that are used most frequently. Because of their different pitch, these may well be employed together in a group, too.

Sound examples: **CD 1 Tr 3**

SITTING POSITION

The player sits astride the cajon with the sound hole to the back and the striking surface to the front. The feet are placed to the sides of the instrument and the cajon is tilted to the back. It is important to keep the back straight and maintain a comfortable position.

The advantage of this sitting position is that the striking surface can be played with more ease. Even the bottom notes in the middle can be reached more easily and the back is strained less.

DRUMMING TECHNIQUES

THE PERUVIAN STYLE

Apart from Cuba, Peru is the one country with the biggest cajon tradition. The Peruvian playing style can be distinguished from the Cuban one by its delicate and direct sound. Similar to the bongo player, the player only uses the first joint of his fingers. At the edge of the cajon, he can produce very high and snappy slaps:

In the bass range, the hand has to form a hollow shape so that only the fingertips hit the striking surface:

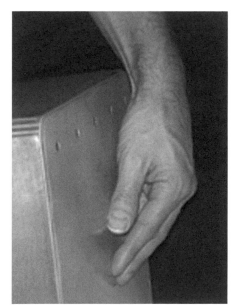

Sound examples: **CD 1 Tr 4**

THE CUBAN STYLE

This playing technique is related to the conga technique and can be transferred to the cajon. The sound is louder, a little more indirect, and the interval from the high pitch (edge) to the low one (bass area) is smaller than for the Peruvian style. The hands slap the striking surface with all fingers and the finger joint:

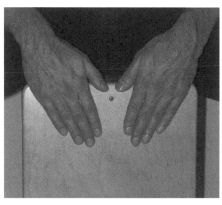

In the bass range, the fingers are used the same way as for the bass tone on the conga, which is that the hands are stretched for the slapping:

Sound examples: **CD 1 Tr 5**

EXTRA TIP:

Like any wood instrument, the cajon is moisture- and heat-sensitive. Great heat as well as moisture can do harm to the instrument. Wood "ages": Play the cajon intensely for 1 to 2 months. Only then the striking surface will have become "soft" and will have developed its full sound. The instrument has strings stretched behind the striking surface, which produces the typically concise snare effect. These strings can be adjusted on the cajon bottom by means of an allen wrench. The following applies here, too: First play with the factory setting and change the string tension only sparsely, if necessary.

SPECIAL SOUNDS AND EFFECTS

GLISSANDO OR SLIDE

The player slightly presses the heel of the right foot against the striking surface while playing on the edge of the cajon:
Now he slowly lifts the foot upwards (keep your balance!) without interrupting his playing. The pitch goes up the more the foot is drawn upwards:

Sound examples: **CD 1 Track 6**

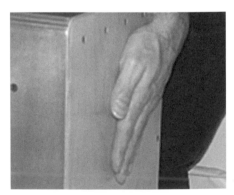

USING THE HEEL AND TIP OF THE FOOT

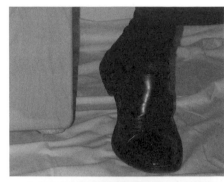

The heel hits the cajon sideways with the tip of the foot staying on the floor and functioning as a pivot (note: This can only be done with shoes or boots).
Sound examples: **CD 1 Tr 7**

THE HAND ON THE SIDE OF THE CAJON

The side areas of the cajon offer an endless number of different sounds. Play on the top edge of the right side with the right hand while the left hand remains on the striking surface:

Sound examples: **CD 1 Tr 8**

WAVE OR FLOATING HAND

This technique originates from conga playing. You need a little patience and persistence to play it but it's worth the effort!
Let your flat hand drop on the center area of the striking surface:

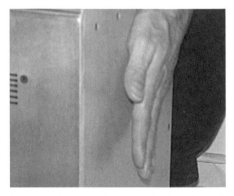

Now lift the front of the hand while the carpus rests on the striking surface.
Let the hand drop again and start all over again:

Sound examples: **CD 1 Tr 9**

BRUSHING TECHNIQUE WITH THUMB AND FINGERS

Place both hands on the striking surface and shape a "W" by spreading out the thumb. Turn the hands outwards with the fingers remaining straight and the thumbs hitting the striking surface:

PLAYING WITH RODS AND BRUSHES

Here it applies as well that you should check out what sounds best and is to your liking.
Important: Rods consist of a bundle of smaller rods. Drum sticks shouldn't be used because these would damage the instrument.

PLAYING WITH THE FINGERNAILS

Form a claw with your hand and hit the striking surface with the fingernails only. The resulting sound is very delicate and rich in overtones. There is an endless number of sound options and playing styles. Discover them yourself!
Everything is permitted!

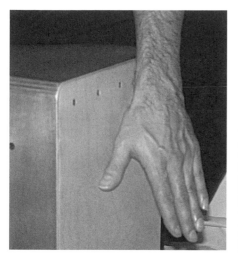

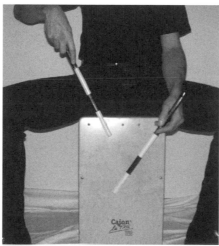

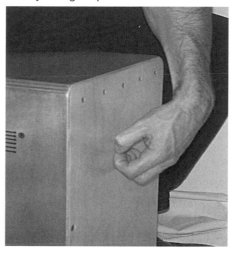

Turn the hands inwards and hit the striking surface with the fingertips:

Sound Examples: **CD 1 Tr 11**

Sound Examples: **CD 1 Tr 13**

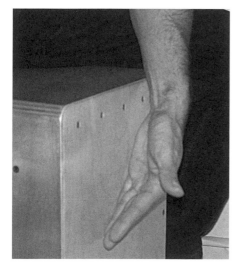

EXTRATIP:

Combine the different variations. The sound examples on the CD will give you an impression of how to apply the described techniques.

Sound examples: CD 1 TR 14

Play with a rod on the side surface and with the hand on the striking surface.

Play with the brushes on the striking surface and use your heel on the side part.

Play with the rods on the striking surface and the heel on the side part.

Sound examples: **CD 1 Tr 10**

Sound examples: **CD 1 Tr 12**

SIGNS AND SYMBOLS

↓ Tip = soft stroke

♪ Open tone = medium stroke

✗ Slap = loud, slapping stroke

R = right hand
L = left hand

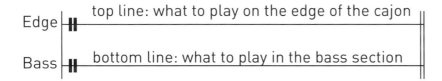

Edge — top line: what to play on the edge of the cajon

Bass — bottom line: what to play in the bass section

  = Exercise

 ♪ = Playalong: This helps to make you enjoy the exercises and rhythms mo
        Mostly, the musical piece has been recorded twice, which means with a
        without rhythm.

① = CD 1

② = CD 2

Tr = Track

Chapter 1:
DYNAMICS

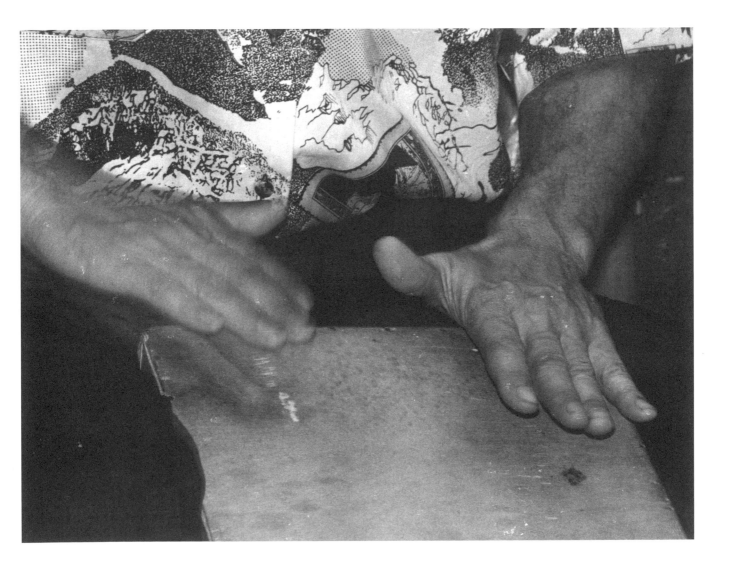

Chapter 1
Dynamics

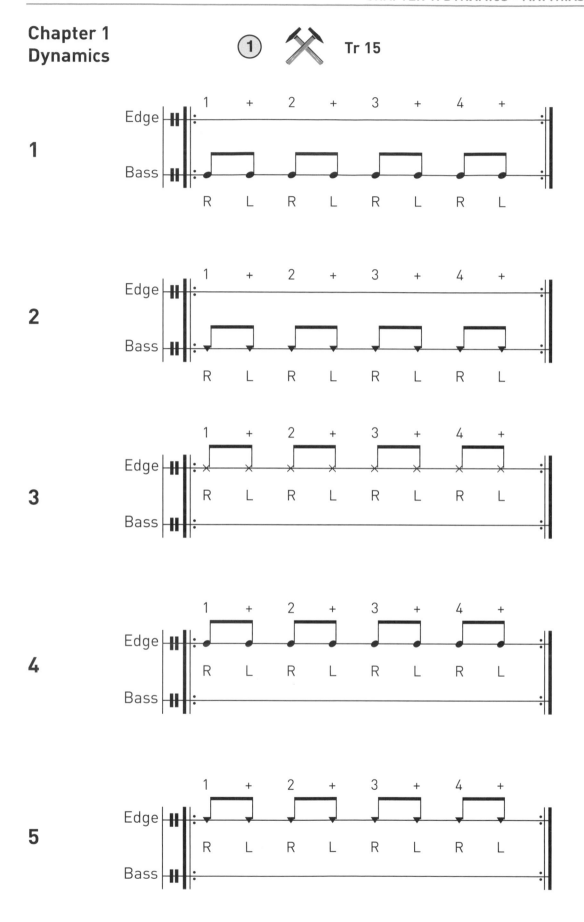

Try to clearly differentiate the different volumes. Make small movements when you play softly and big ones when you play loudly. Be relaxed and play out of your whole arm and not only from the movements of the wrists.

Chapter 2:
HAND PATTERNS-STICKINGS

Chapter 2
Hand Patterns-Stickings

 Tr 16

1

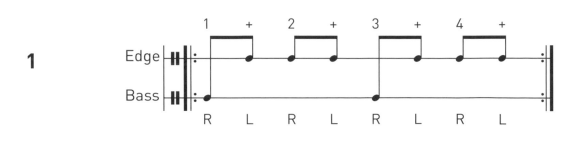

2

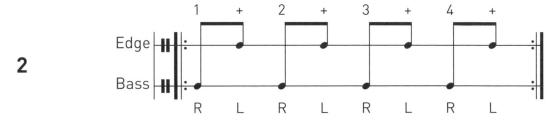

3

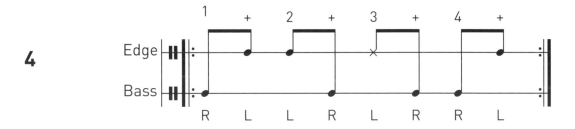

4

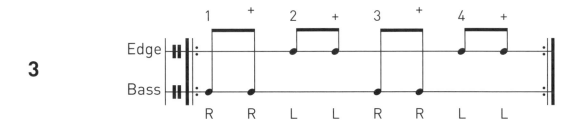

5

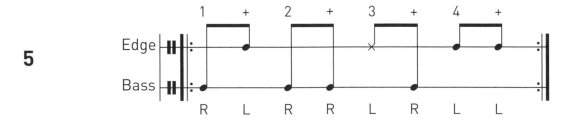

Chapter 2
Hand Patterns-Stickings

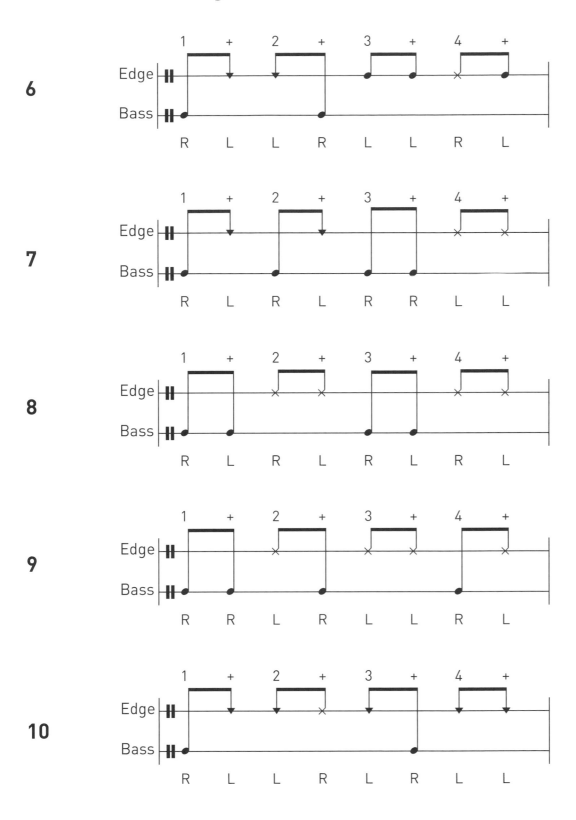

Some of these hand patterns have been taken from the drums. They are meant to help you make your playing more variable. Start practicing slowly and with a metronome, if possible (tempo 60-80 bpm).

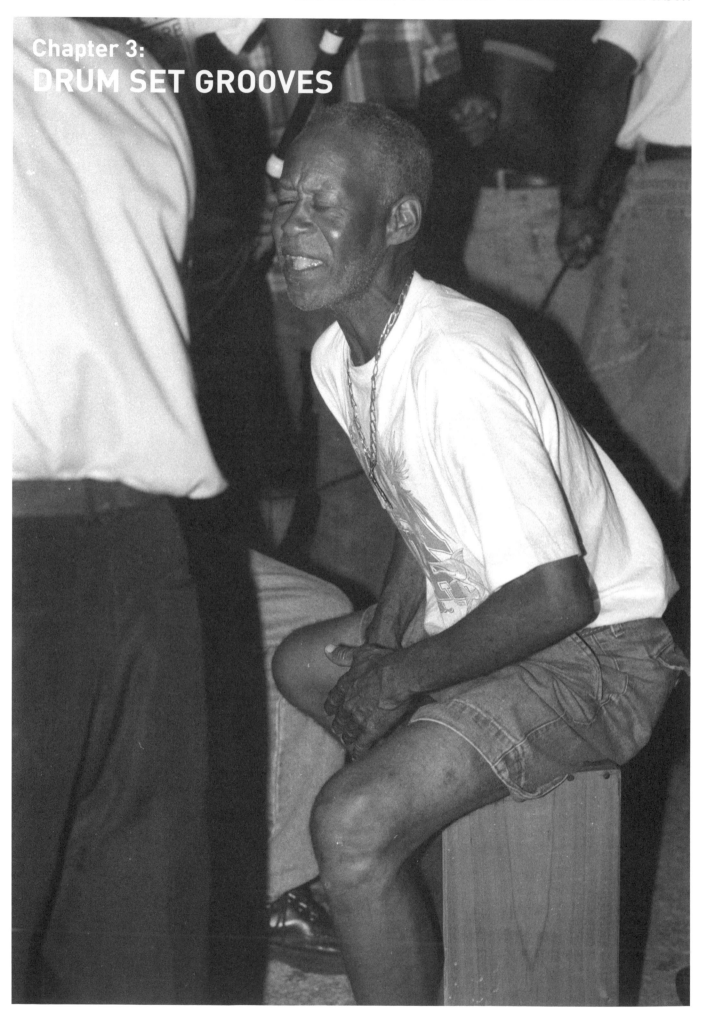

Chapter 3:
DRUM SET GROOVES

Chapter 3
Drum Set Grooves

(1) Tr 15

(1) Tr 18

(1) Tr 19

(1) Tr 20

(1) Tr 21

Sound like a small drum set. The bass is to replace the big drum and the edge tone the small drum of the set. These rhythms are especially suited as accompaniment for pop and rock songs.

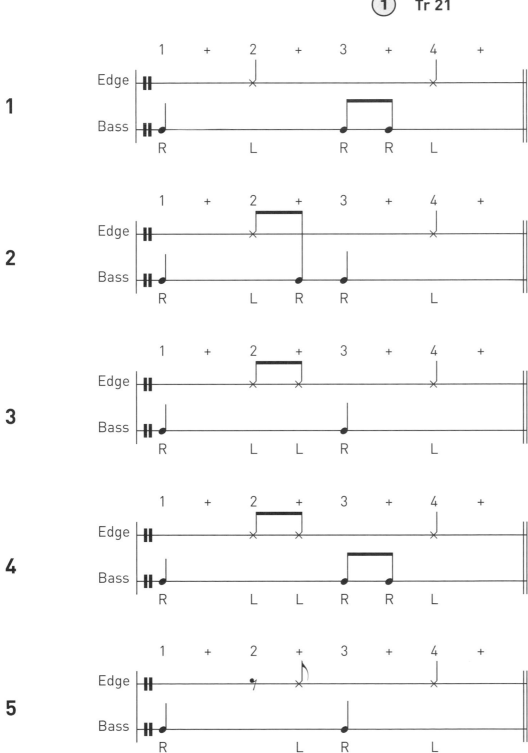

Chapter 3
Drum Set Grooves

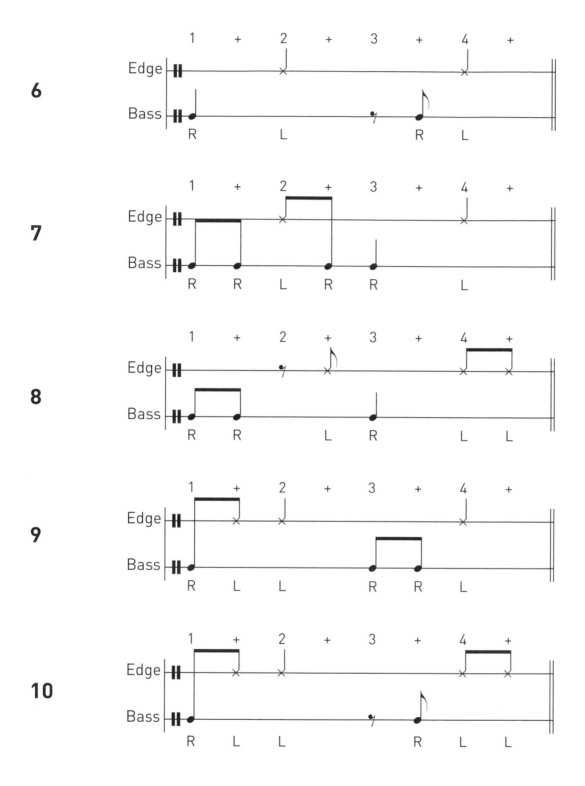

Chapter 4:
DRUM SET GROOVES WITH 1/8 OSTINATO

Chapter 4
Drum Set Grooves

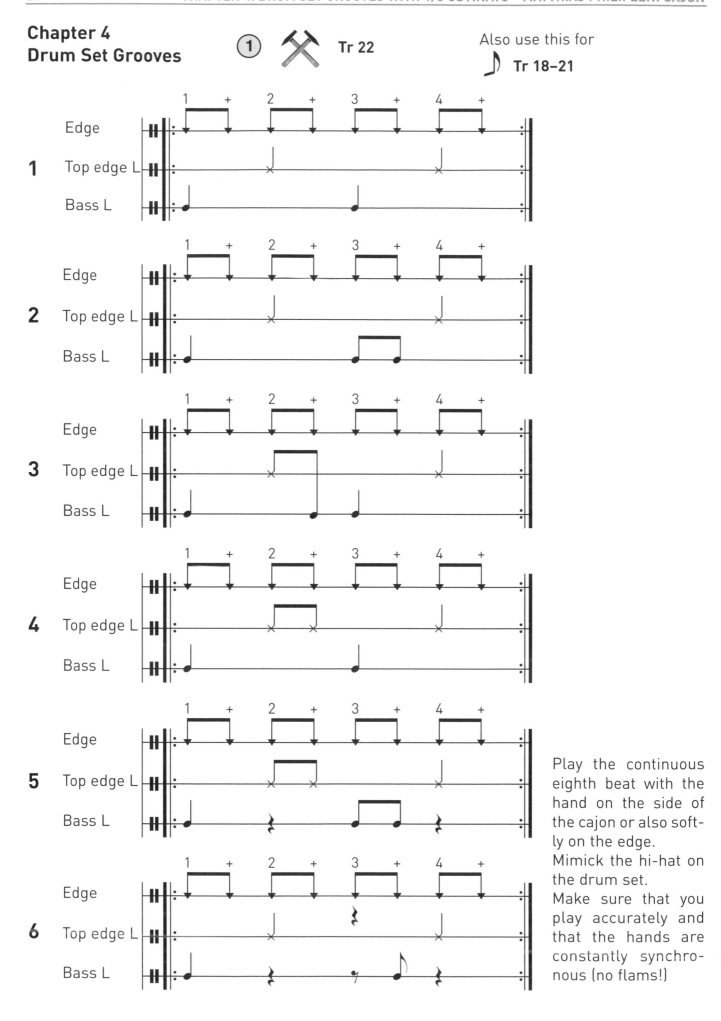

Play the continuous eighth beat with the hand on the side of the cajon or also softly on the edge.
Mimick the hi-hat on the drum set.
Make sure that you play accurately and that the hands are constantly synchronous (no flams!)

Chapter 5:
DRUMSET GROOVES WITH 1/16 OSTINATO

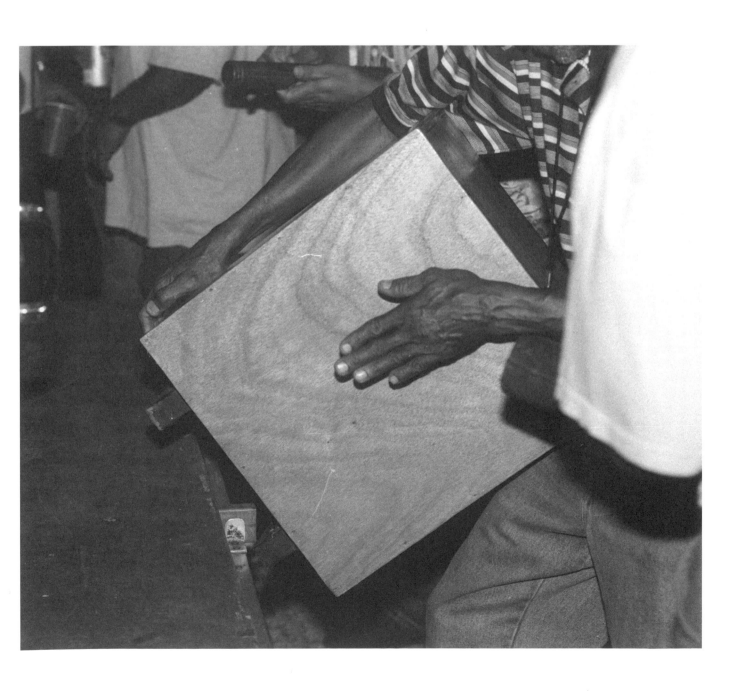

Chapter 5
Drum Set Grooves

 Tr 23    Tr 24–25

Again, make sure that you're playing accurately. Don' t start too quickly!

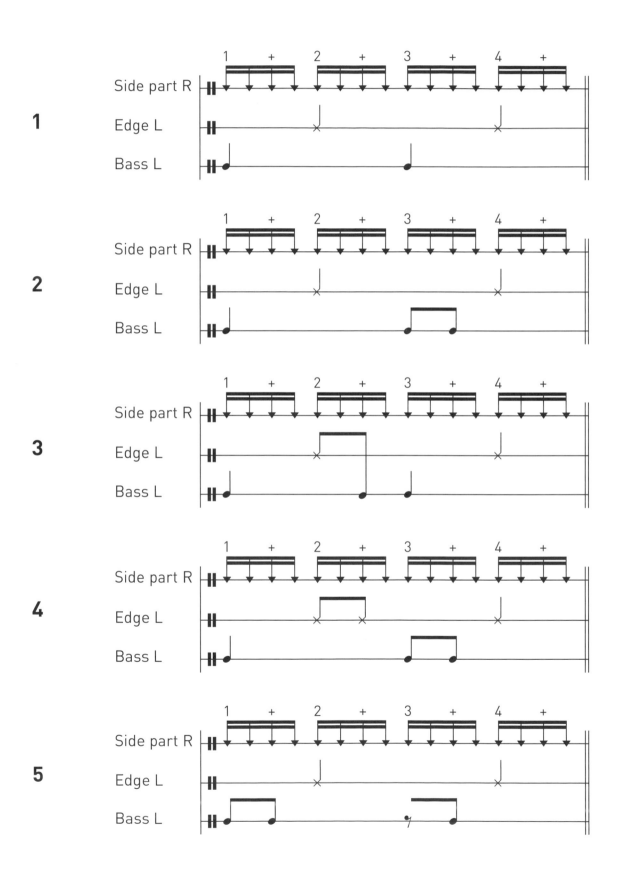

Chapter 5
Drum Set Grooves

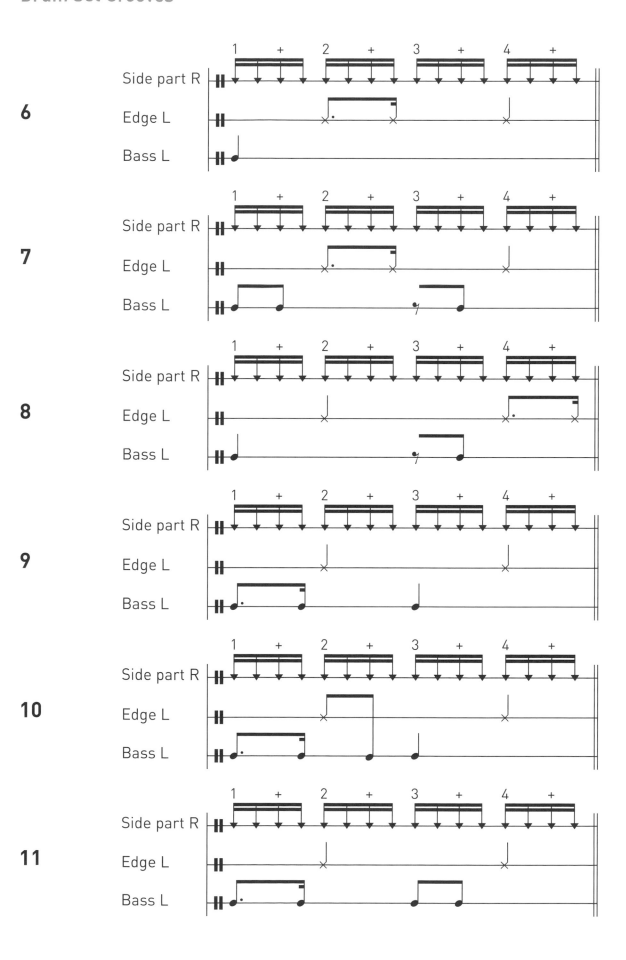

Chapter 5
Drum Set Grooves

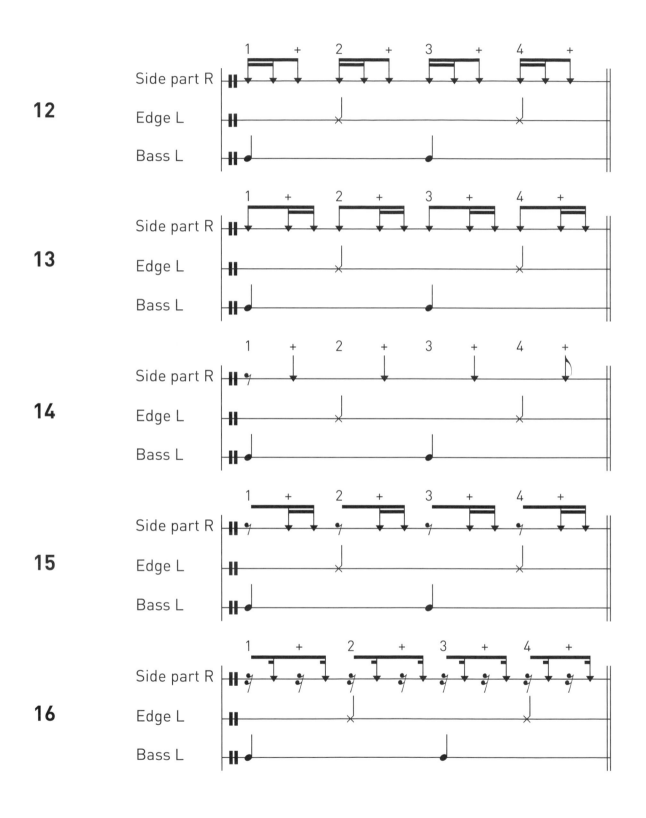

Chapter 6:
ACCENT EXERCISES

Chapter 6
Accent Exercises

1

2

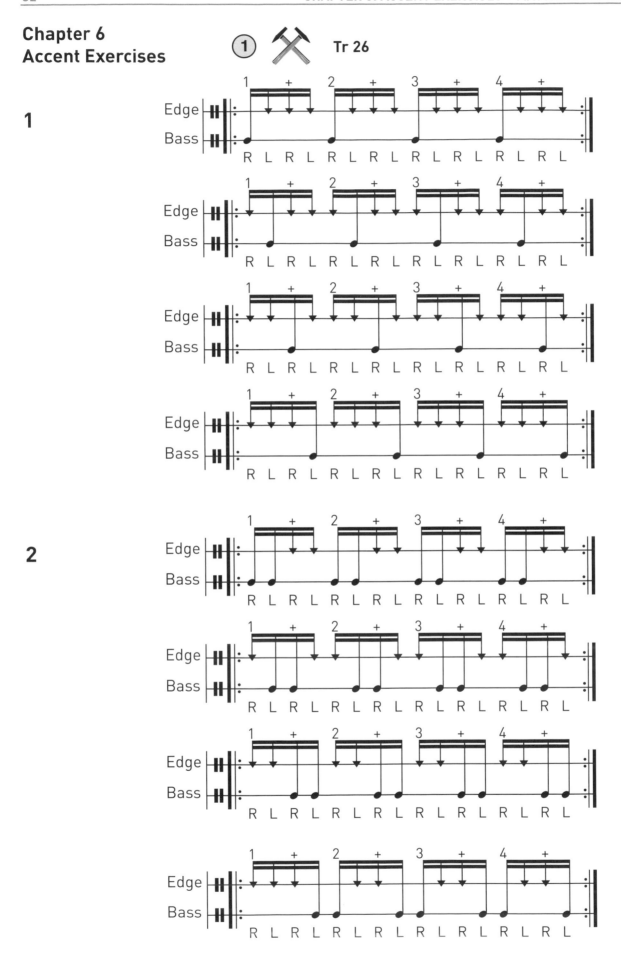

Now a little challenge for your weaker left hand. Practice every line at first slowly and separately, then try playing all 4 lines in one go. The accents of both hands should be dynamically equal.

Chapter 6
Accent Exercises

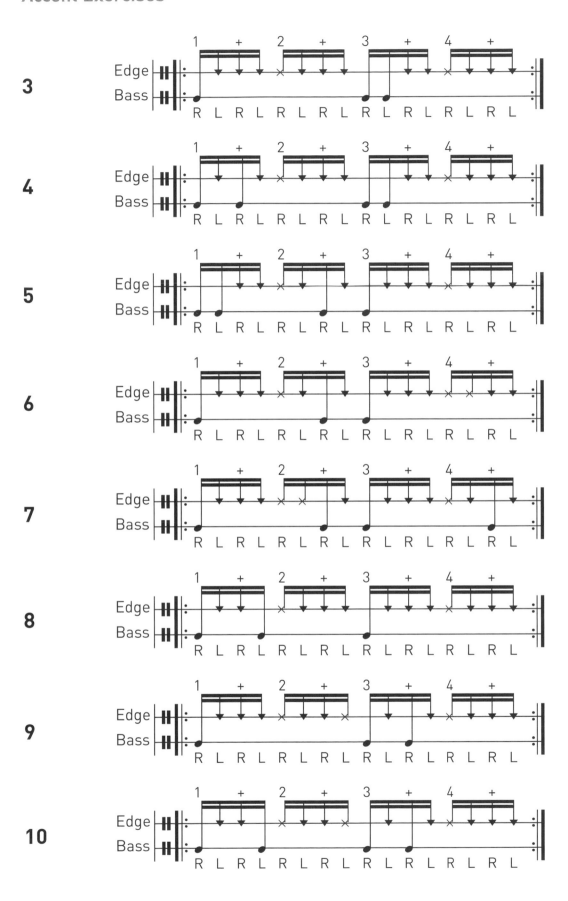

Chapter 7:
SIXTEENTH NOTE RHYTHMS WITH R–L HAND PATTERN (FLOW)

Chapter 7
Sixteenth Note Rhythms With R-L Hand Pattern (Flow)

 Tr 27

The listed rhythms equally employ both hands. Always try to maintain the flow of soft and loud strokes. Start slowly again (60 bpm).

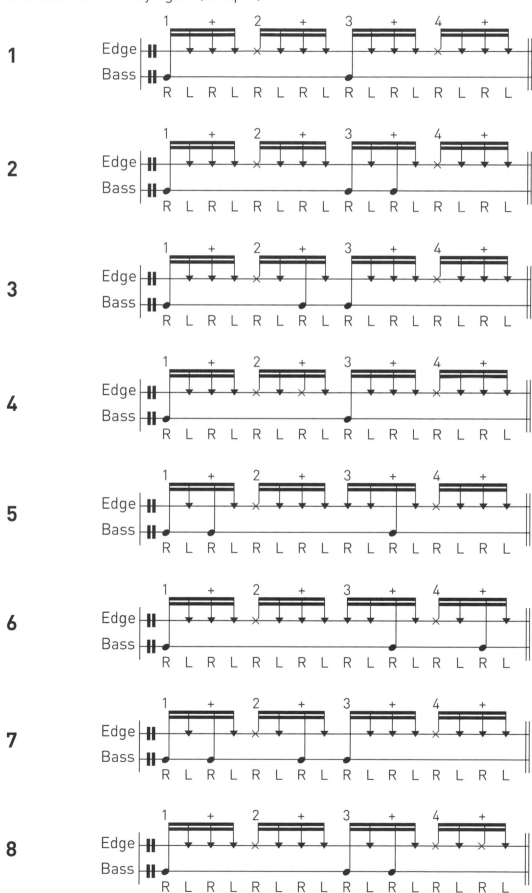

Chapter 7
Sixteenth Note Rhythms With R-L Hand Pattern (Flow)

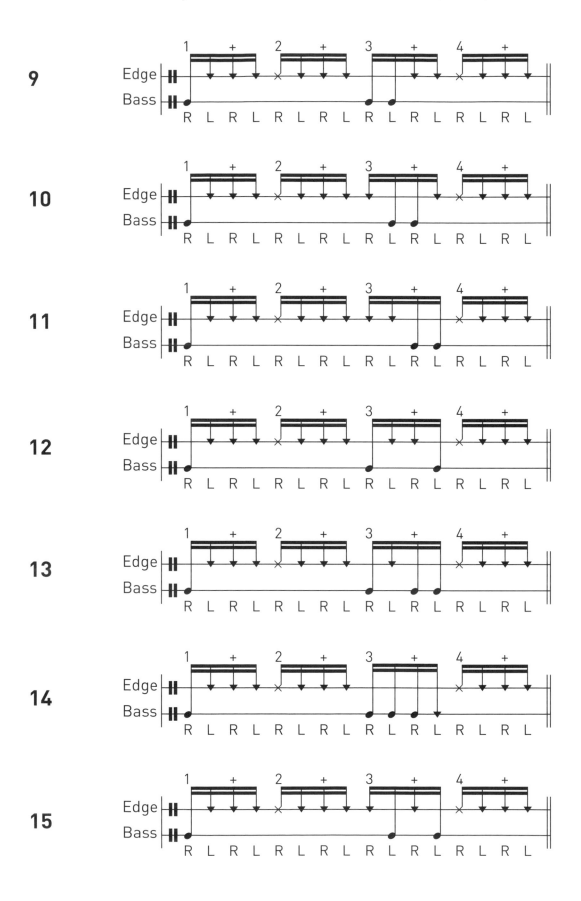

Chapter 7
Sixteenth Note Rhythms With R-L Hand Pattern (Flow)

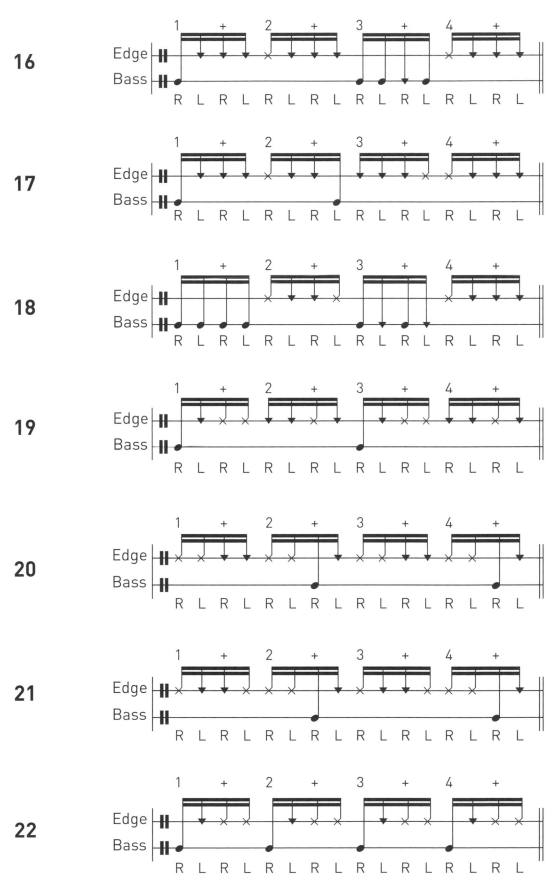

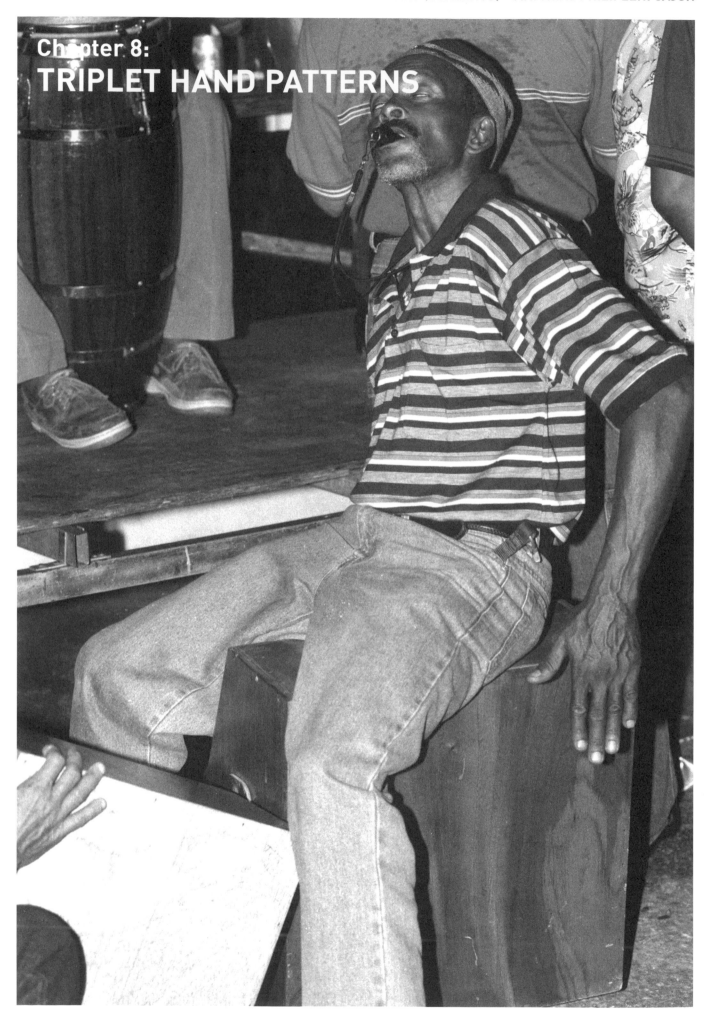

Chapter 8:
TRIPLET HAND PATTERNS

Chapter 8
Triplet Hand Patterns (Stickings)

 Tr 28   Tr 29

Here you learn different hand patterns again. This time, the triplet is our basis (three counts per beat). The first exercise is in the waltz style and will help you develop the right feel.

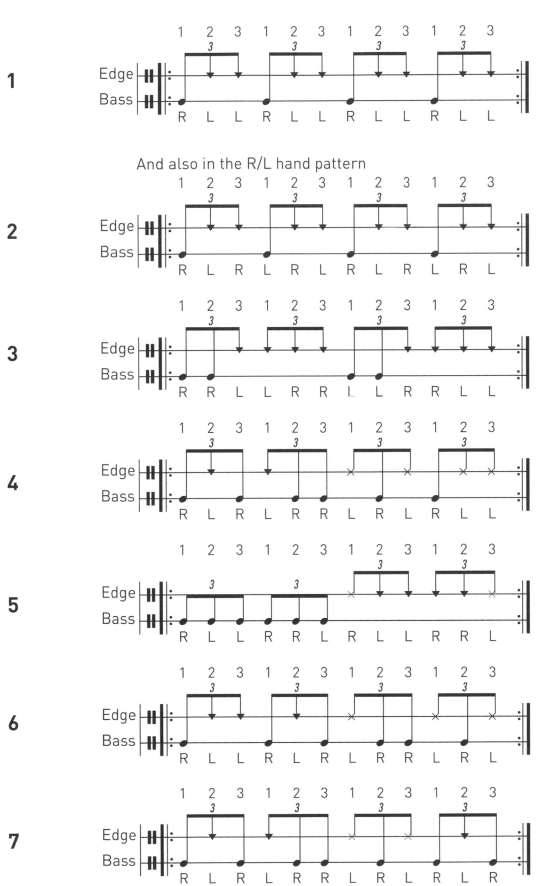

Chapter 8
Triplet Rhythms (Grooves)

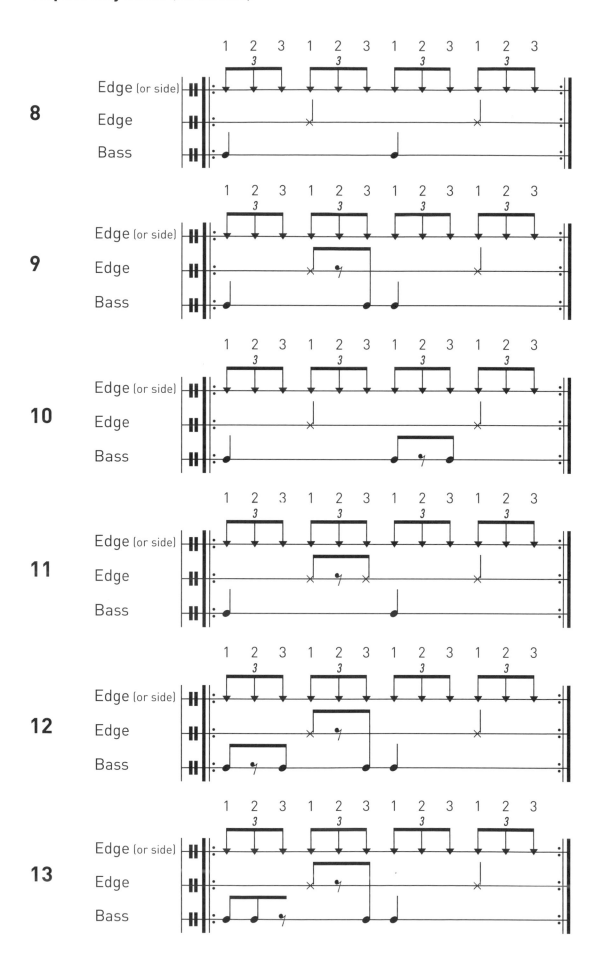

Chapter 9:
SHUFFLE RHYTHMS

Chapter 9
Shuffle Rhythms

Based on the triplet, you will learn to play the shuffle figure which is missing the second eighth note in the middle. First count three eighth notes to learn where the two beats should be placed correctly.

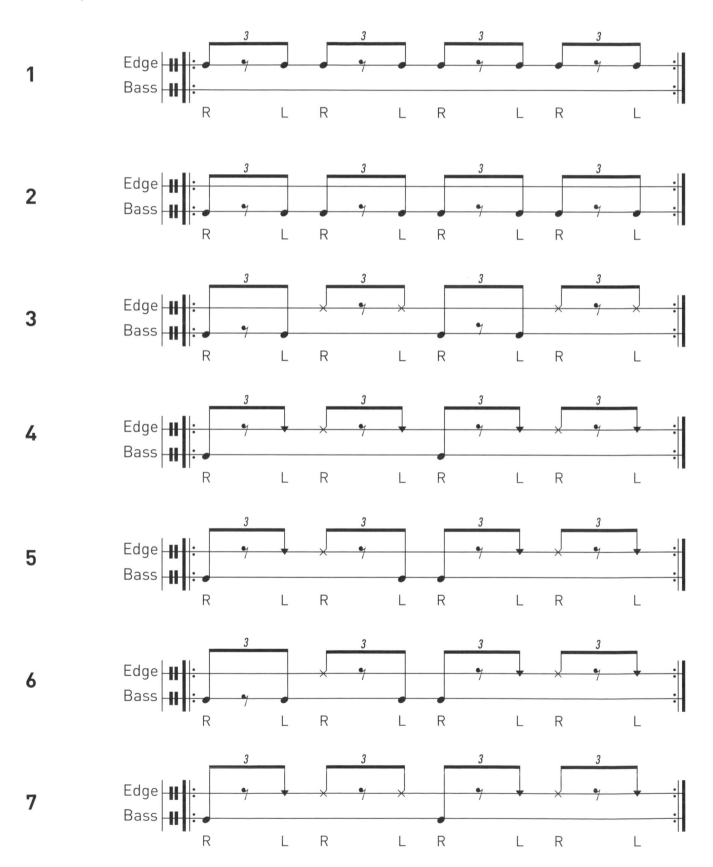

Chapter 9
Shuffle Rhythms

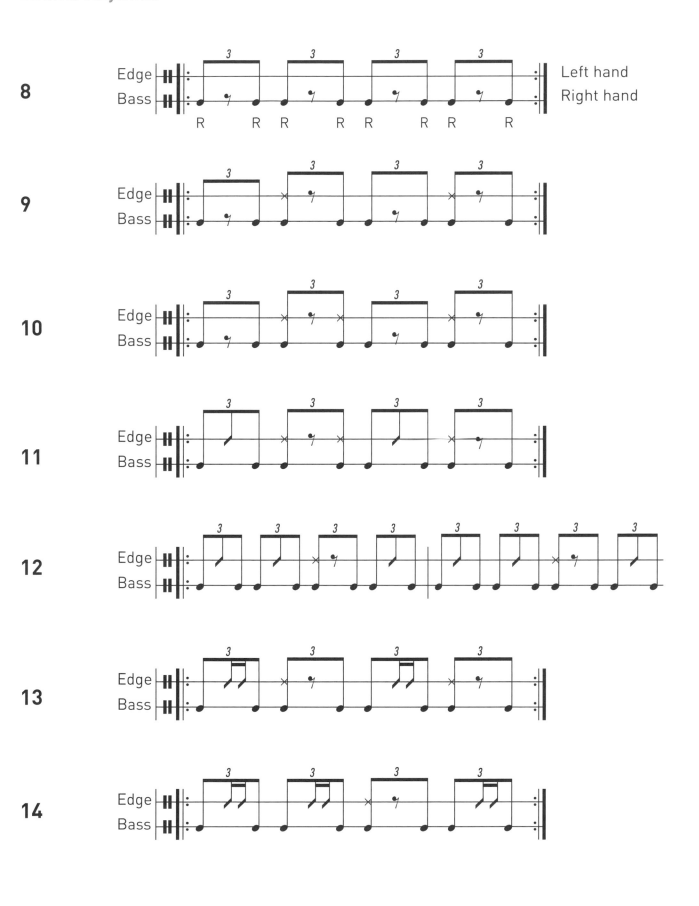

Chapter 9
Shuffle Halftime

Basic:

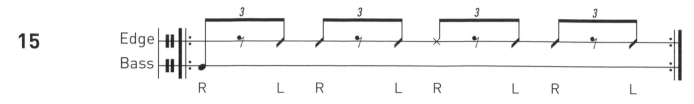

A two-measure rhythm:

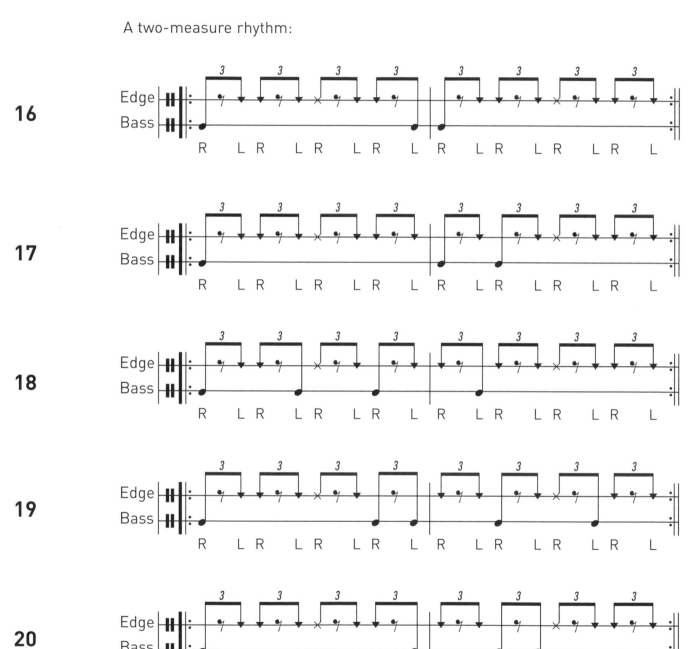

Chapter 10:
SHAKER GROOVES

Chapter 10
Shaker Grooves

 Tr 33

Shaker
to the front →

Shaker
to the back ←

Try to move the shaker in a horizontal position. Hold the wrist rigid and play from the elbow. Make sure that the shaker motion is short, defined and bouncy. Achieve more effects by closing your hand and thus muting the shaker additionally.

Chapter 11:
CAJINTO GROOVES

Chapter 11
Cajinto Grooves

I have played the following 11 grooves on the booster setup (www.schlag-werk.com).

Half of the cajinto's striking surface is not smooth, which means it can be played well with brushes.

The bass cajon is mounted on a floor panel and is struck with a special beater. As the cajon, this setup is a fantastic alternative to the common drum set.

Chapter 11
Cajinto Grooves

 Tr 1

Bossa Nova

Right hand with brush (cajinto)

Left hand with rod (cajinto)

Bass cajon + hi-hat, closed

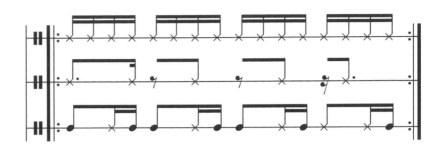

In the sound example, the brush figure of the right hand is being brushed first. In the second example, it is being struck.

Samba

Basic figure (played with a brush)

Tr 2

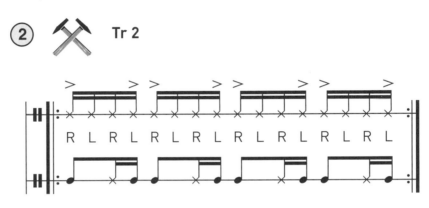

Baiao

Tr 3

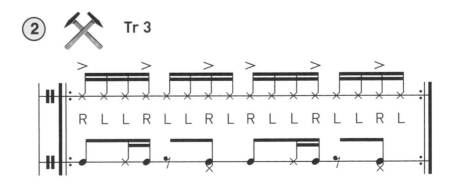

Chapter 11
Cajinto Grooves

  Tr 4

Cascara, Clave und Tumbao Bass

Both hands (cajinto)

Hi-hat
+
Bass cajon, kicked

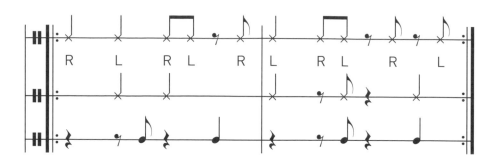

Both hands play the cascara figure using the (RLRL) hand pattern.

The left foot plays a 2-3 son clave on the hi-hat.

The bass cajon plays the tumbao bass (right foot)

Swing

 Tr 5

Right hand (cajinto)

Left hand (cajinto)

Hi-hat, kicked

Bass-Drum
softly with heel down

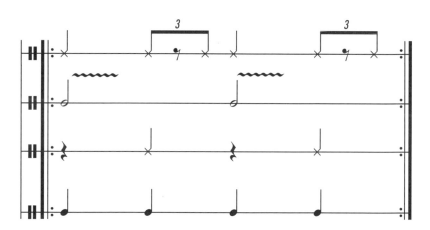

The right hand plays the swing figure, the left brushes in circles without accentuation, the hi-hat is kicked on 2 and 4.

Chapter 11
Cajinto Grooves

Hip Hop
Basic figure

Cajinto
Bass-Cajon

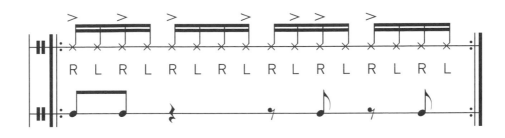

New
Orleans
Basic figure

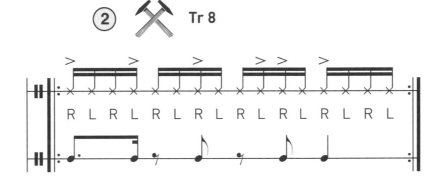

Similar to the shuffle, always keep a highly swinging playing style in mind for the sixteenth notes when you play Hip Hop and New Orleans.

Shuffle Up-Time
Basic figure

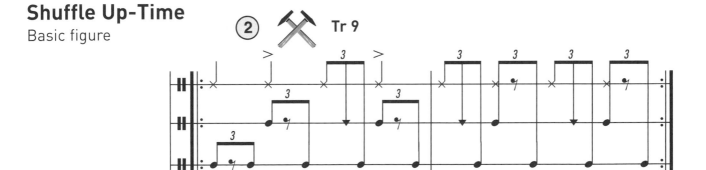

Chapter 11
Cajinto Grooves

 Tr 10

Pop

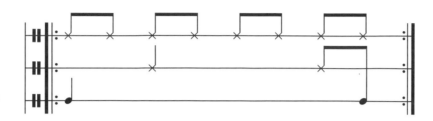

Hi-hat
Cajinto
Bass cajon

 Tr 11

Songo

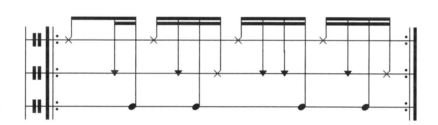

Hi-hat
Cajinto
Bass cajon

 Tr 12

Soca

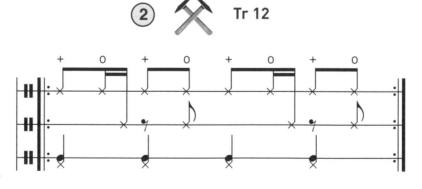

Hi-hat
Cajinto
Bass cajon
and Hi-hat,
kicked

+ = Hi-hat closed
o = Hi-hat open

STYLES

African Shuffle

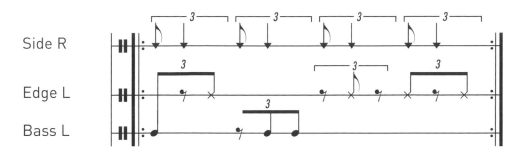

African Shuffle: A rhythmic figure originating in African music. Think in groups of three (triplets) as for the known shuffle, but omit the last eighth note. (In the common shuffle, this is the second eighth note.) This creates a driving, swinging pulse which never sounds static.

Alea Six

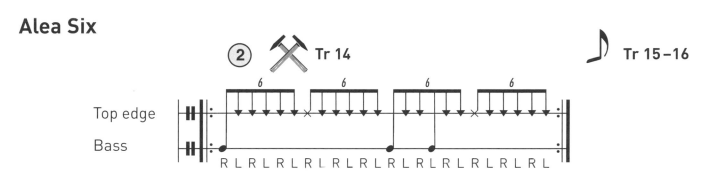

Alea Six: A 6/8 rhythm which I played for a song of the band ALEA. It contains compa elements (flamenco) and its R-L sequence of strokes makes it very light and dance-like.

Blues

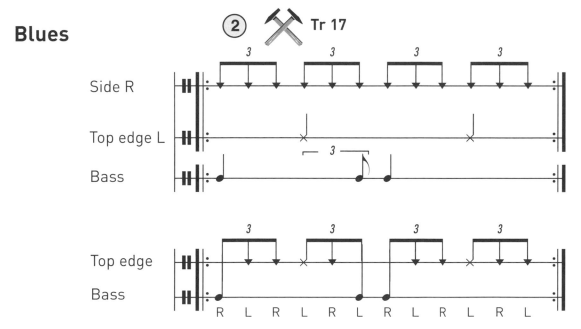

Blues: This significant musical form emerged in the Afro-American population in the southern states of the US at the end of the 19th and the beginning of the 20th century. This style was significant for the development of jazz, rock, soul and even hip hop. It often expresses a melancholy, sad attitude towards life.

STYLES

Samba

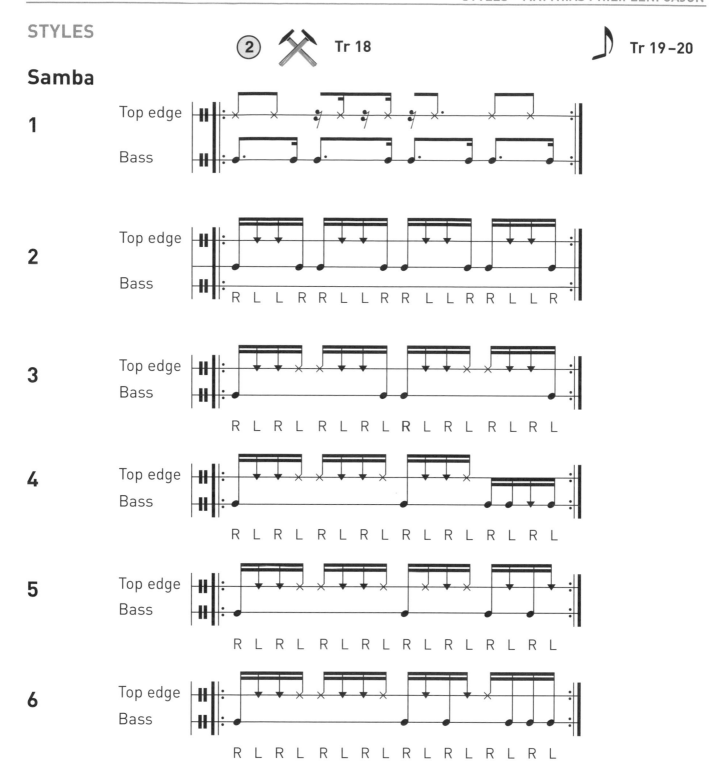

Samba:
Originally a dance, which was brought over by African slaves to their new home Brazil. Today it is probably the most popular rhythm in Latin music. Listen to records by Brazilian artists (Gilberto Gil, Milton Nascimento, Djavan, Baden Powell, Joao Gilberto, Luiz Bonfa, Antonio Carlos Jobim, Sergio Mendez) to get a feel for this musical style.

STYLES

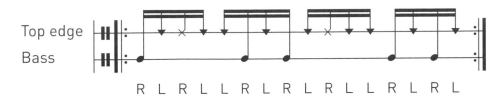

Partido Alto

Partido Alto: A rhythmical figure that corresponds to the clave. Just like the clave in Afro-Cuban music, the partido alto serves as a kind of "code" for Brazilian music. The well-defined structure is frequently used in samba variations.

Bossa Nova
Preparatory Exercises

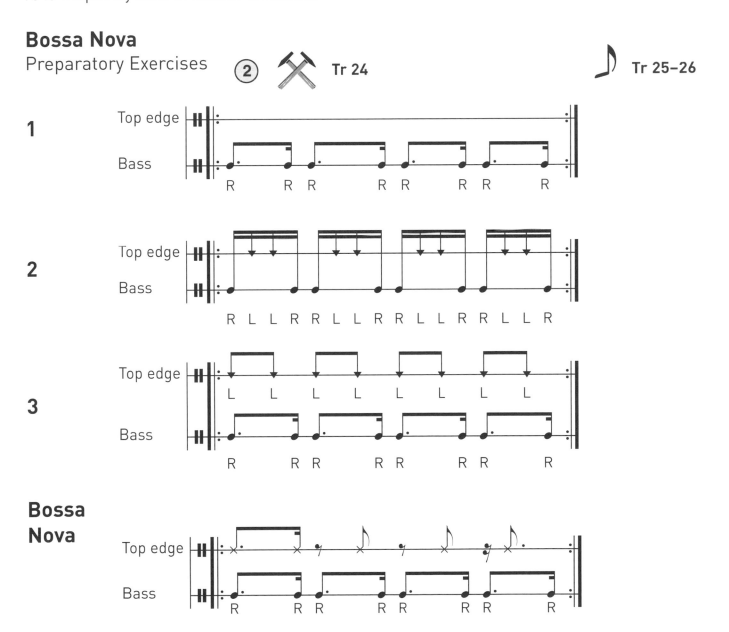

Bossa Nova

Bossa Nova: "New Wave", a musical form which was derived from the samba in the 1950s and 1960s. Very slow and with sparse instrumentation, it is one of the best-known and mostly-used rhythms in jazz, pop and Latin music.

STYLES

Hip Hop

Hip Hop: originates from soul and funk. A music form that came up in the 1970s, emerged especially in New York and uses rap and scratching.
Play these rhythms dance-like, light and swinging. Pay attention to loud and heavy accents.

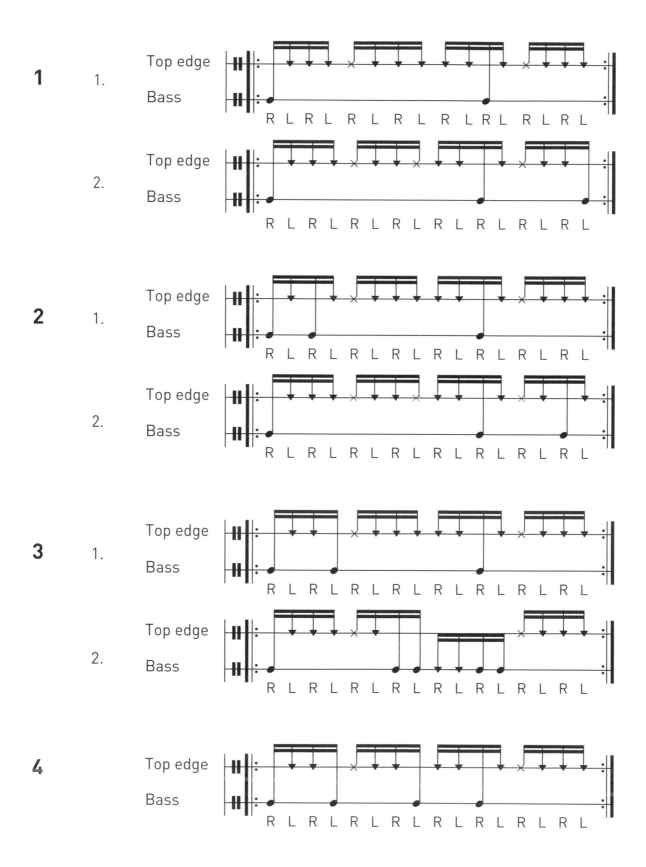

STYLES

Hip Hop

5   1.
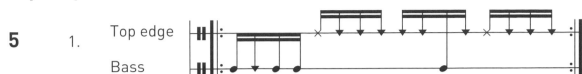

2.

6   1.
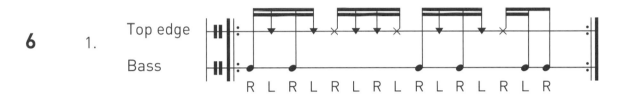

2.
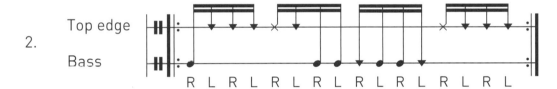

7   1.
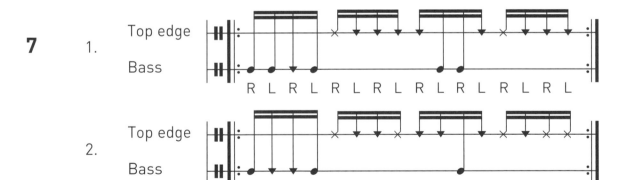

2.

8

New Orleans

New Orleans: This is the antecedent of jazz, a buoyant kind of music which emerged in the city and region of the same name. It lives on its swing feel and in the beginning it was played with a small instrumentation for festive events. For this, the band often marched in the second line (second line music) behind the bride and groom or behind the coffin at a funeral.

Preparatory

1

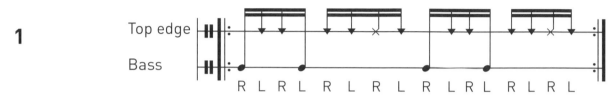

2

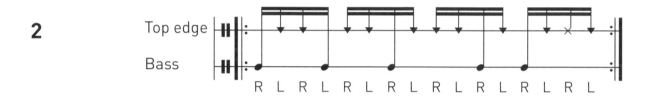

3

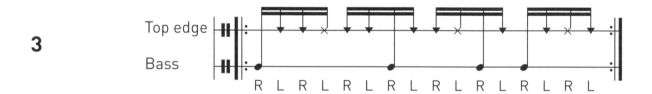

4

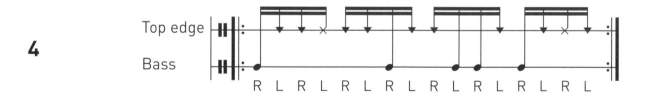

5

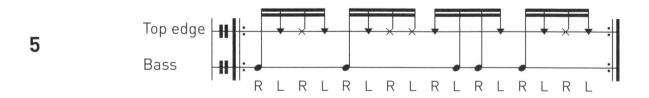

STYLES

New Orleans

6

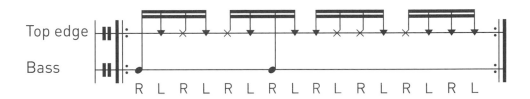

Top edge
Bass

R L R L R L R L R L R L R L R L

7

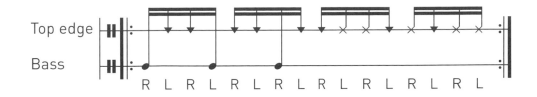

Top edge
Bass

R L R L R L R L R L R L R L R L

STYLES

 **Tr 32** **Tr 33**

Country

1

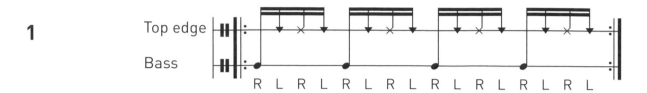

Chicken Pick

2

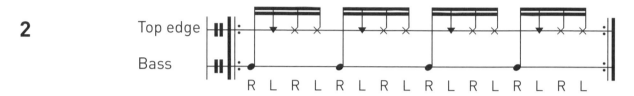

Country: emerged in the USA in the early 20th century from the music of the European immigrants, especially the English and Irish. Johnny Cash, Hank Williams, but also Garth Brooks and many others knew how to lift this rather plain music style to an international popularity by adding pop and rock elements. Play these rhythms in a light and swinging manner. Originally, the rhythm pattern comes from the guitar.

Rumba de Flamenco

Tr 34 **Tr 35–36**

1

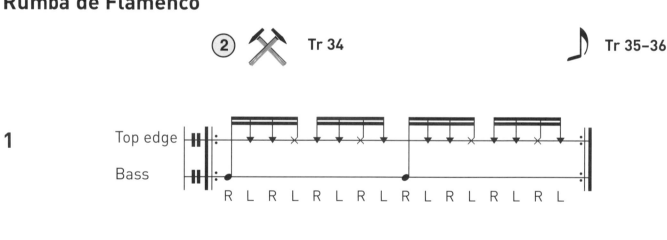

2

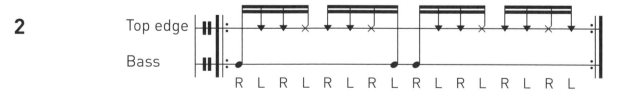

Rumba de Flamenco: a flamenco music style. It became known in the 1980s by bands such as the Gipsy Kings and later Chico and the Gipsys. This is a driving 4/4 rhythm. So make your accents clear and pay attention to flowing, soft strokes as well. Just as in flamenco music, the temperament, the dance element as well as the energy are crucial.

STYLES

Martillo

Martillo: the hammer, an Afro-Cuban bongo rhythm that is often used as a basic pattern. I have used it for the cajon. Make sure to play loud and snapping slaps on the edge. In addition, you may phrase the martillo the Peruvian way, which means with your fingertips only.

Compas

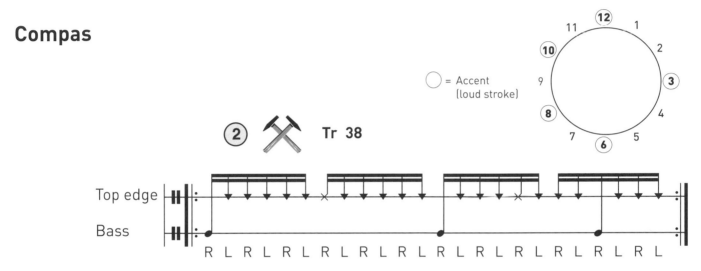

Compas: describes a cycle. Starting on the 12th beat, you play all figures like on a clock-face until you come back to 12. In musical notation, this would be a 12/8 rhythm. Flamenco music has used the image of the cycle (disk) for many years to explain the continuously repeated pulse. First, start by clapping the beat as displayed in the clock above. The circled numbers are clapped loudly. Count out loud, starting on (12) .

Buleria

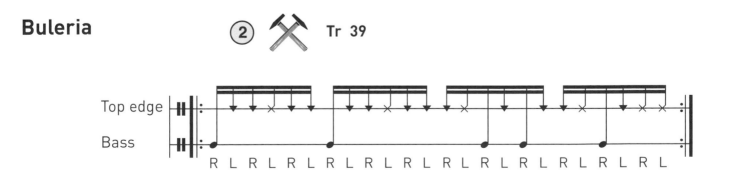

Buleria: Based on the flamenco-clock, this is a dance that is performed in a fresh and energetic way. Notice the additional accents. Always start slowly and count out loud.

 **Tr 40**  **Tr 41–42**

Baiao

1

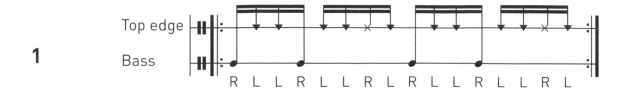

2

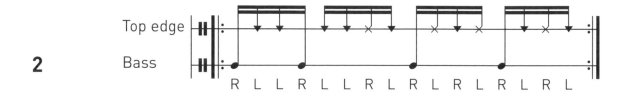

3

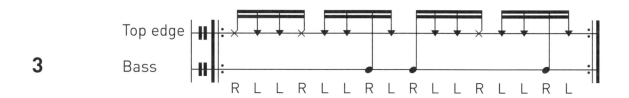

Baiao: a Brazilian dance and at the same time one of the most significant rhythms of this country. It emerged around 1840 in Bahia and is almost as popular as the samba.

Merengue

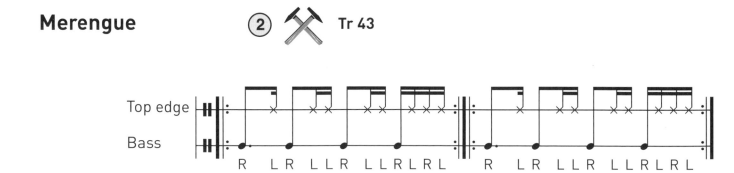

Merengue: a South-American music style originating from Haiti, Puerto Rico and the Dominican Republic. The rhythm is played fast and driving (120-180 bpm). It still has an immense impact on nowadays music because of electronic music and its blending with hip hop, house and techno.

STYLES
Reggae

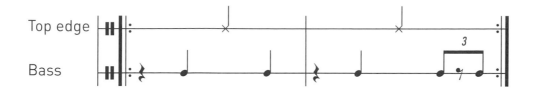

Reggae: emerged at the beginning of the 1960s from various musical styles such as R&B, soul, jazz and country. Bob Marley, who lived in Jamaica, made this musical style famous all over the world. I have notated two basic rhythms. The first reggae rhythm is minimalist and sparse and mostly accompanies the verse. Use the so-called "stepper grooves" in the chorus. The continuous bass figure in quarter notes provides the groove with a very dance-like element.

Reggae "Steppers"

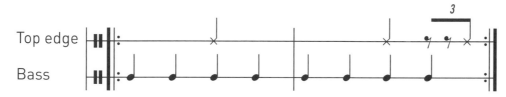

Reggae "Steppers" Variation

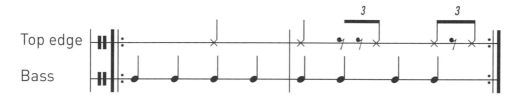

Soca

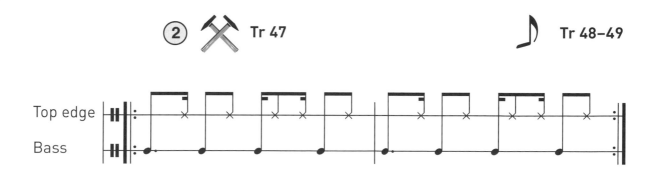

Soca: This is a music of the Caribbean Islands. In the early 1970s, the calypso was combined with Indian rhythms and this is where the name SOCA comes from = soul of calypso.
This groove is played fast, too, and is used especially often for carnival parties in the Caribbean.

Salsa
Cascara

(2) ⚒ **Tr 50**   ♪ **Tr 51–52**

Right hand

Clave (2–3)

Left hand

Application

1   Edge (or side) R

Edge L

Bass

Cascara

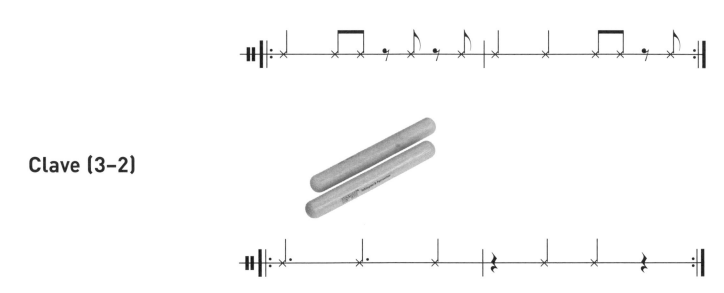

Clave (3–2)

Salsa: This is a musical form that emerged in the early 1960s. The pioneer of this Latin style was Tito Puento's piano-player, Eddie Palmieri. He reduced the Latin orchestra that had previously been large to a small orchestration with piano, congas, bongos, vocals and trombone as the sole wind instrument. In addition, he worked in his compositions with jazz elements and improvisation. Salsa is a quite popular dance style today.

The cascara is a figure that was originally struck on the shell of timbales. It is connected to the clave (key) and will be displayed in the following figures. I have confined myself to the two variations of the son clave.

STYLES

Application

2

Edge (or side) R
Edge L
Bass

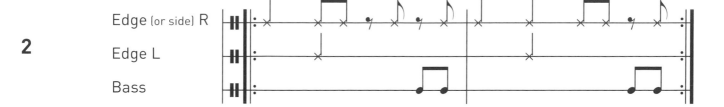

Cascara in R-L Sticking

R L R L R L R L R L

Application

3

Edge (or side)
Bass

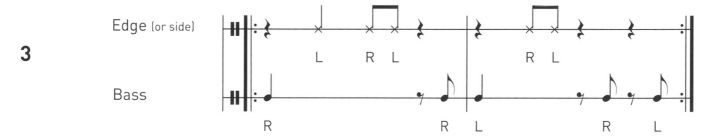

Techno

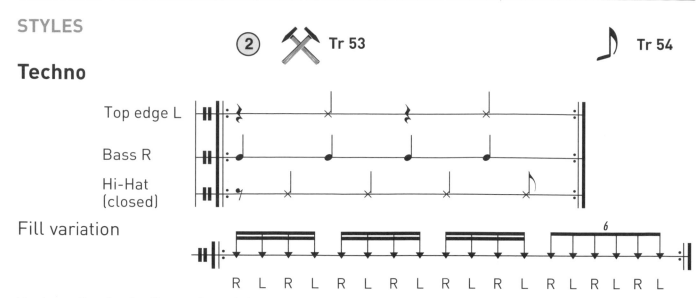

Techno: Synthetically produced dance music that emerged at the end of the 1980s. Its goal was to use the machine as a new sound source. Industry sounds and noises were recorded in a sequence and mixed with a heavy 4/4 bass drum beat and a minimum of chord and melody structures. This style has developed further over the years and many different sub-forms such as jungle, drum'n'bass and house have evolved.

Jungle

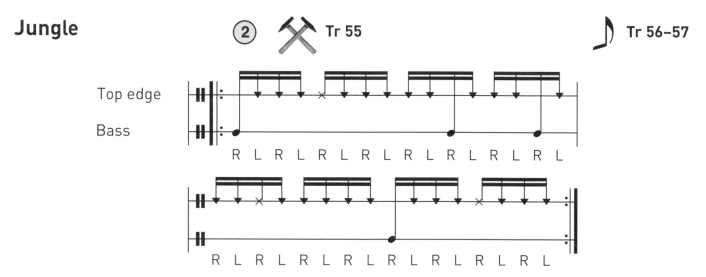

Jungle: This music evolved in England in the early 1990s. Its tempo is 170 bpm and it includes funk and techno elements. Sparse beats are often enriched by so-called break beats (syncopated rhythm fragments). As with drum and bass, it is a great challenge for us to transfer these rapid electronic grooves to the instrument.

Drum 'n Bass

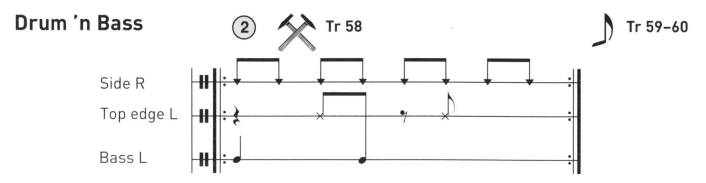

Drum and Bass: style that emerged from jungle. It is played with an even higher tempo (up to 190 bpm) and thus meets the requirements of today's dance music that is getting faster and faster. Compared to jungle, the grooves are arranged more simply. The high tempo and half-time bass lines create a constant friction for the listener, which is exactly what makes this music attractive.

STYLES

Odd Meter

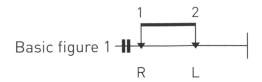

Basic figure 1

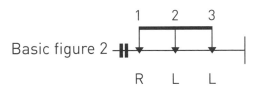

Basic figure 2

Odd meter: For Western Europeans it is not easy to listen to other meters, so-called odd meters, than the common ones of 4/4, 3/4 or 6/8 time. Our ears are simply not used to these. Therefore, I have tried to facilitate the counting and thus the understanding of these rhythms for you.

With the groups of three or four beats you are able to play any considerable rhythm. In addition, it will be easier for you to produce a continuous counting flow. The following examples show some of these groups and how to apply them. Be creative and come up with your own rhythms based on this information. The possibilities are endless!

First rhythms and combination of the basic figures

Count

1 ② ✗ Tr 61

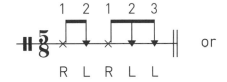   or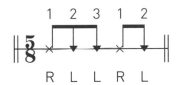

2 ② ✗ Tr 62

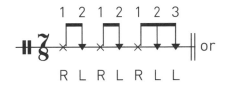   or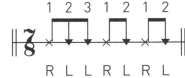

and

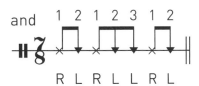

3 ② ✗ Tr 63

4 ② ✗ Tr 64

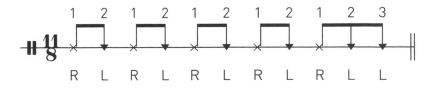
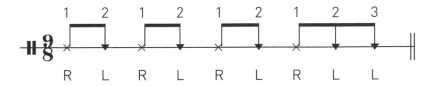

STYLES

Odd Meter

Applying the basic figures

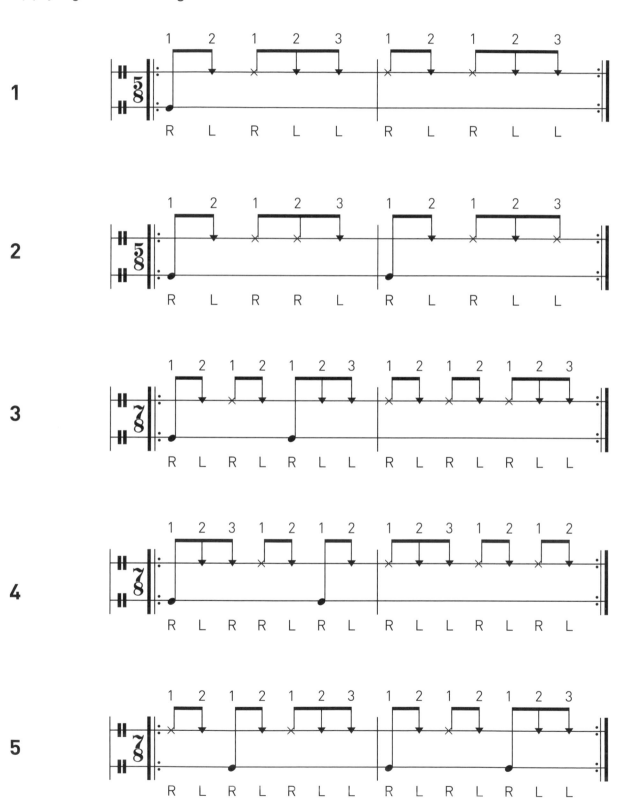

STYLES

Odd Meter

1

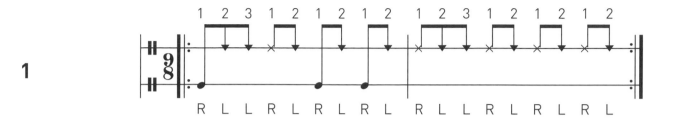

2

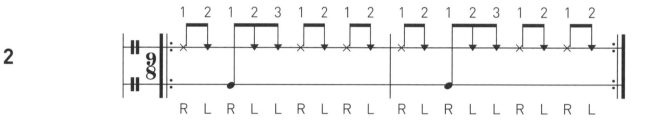

3

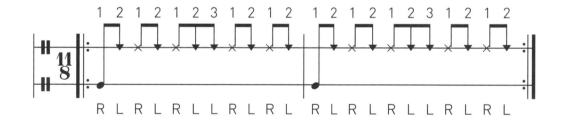

4

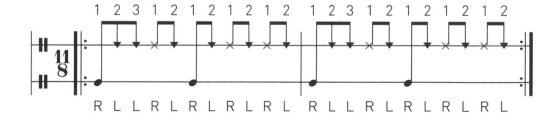

② ⚒ Tr 65   ♪ Tr 66–67

Di Bango Six

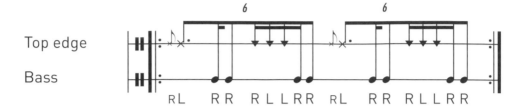

Di Bango Six: I got the inspiration for this rhythm from a recording by saxophone-player Mani Di Bango. It is not difficult to recognize this musician's African roots. The bass figure forms an ostinato over which, after a little practice, you may solo.

Funk

② ⚒ Tr 68

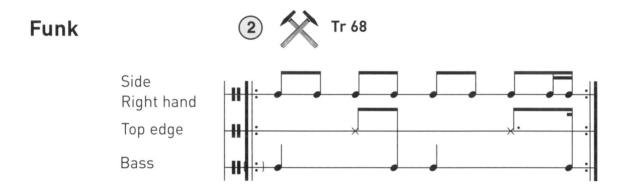

Funk: indicates the dance music of the Afro-American population at the end of the 1960s. Strongly influenced by jazz, rhythm & blues and soul elements, this music has survived to the present day and shaped other musical styles. James Brown is commonly referred to as one of the most significant funk musicians. Always play the beat accentuated and perform the groove with a drive and very "angular".

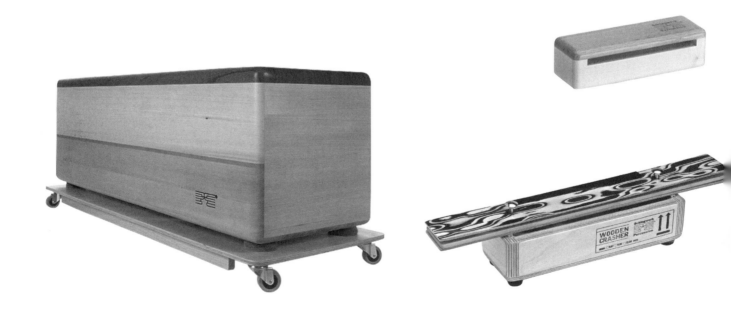

STYLES

Peruvian Twelve

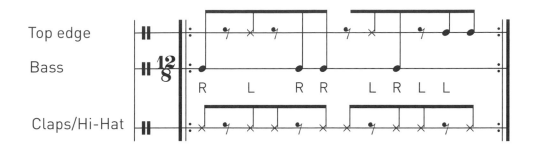

Peruvian Six: the basis of the musica negra from Peru. The common folk music there has always used the cajon as a rhythm instrument. To the present day, this music style has not lost any of its popularity and is presented even in Europe by musicians such as Susana Baca.

Swing

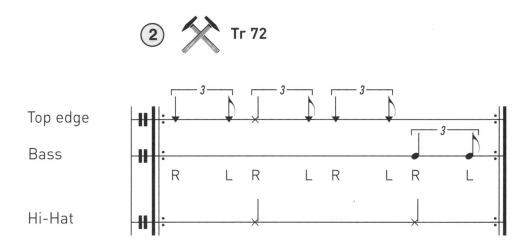

Swing: This was the dance music of America in the 1930s. Many other styles have been inspired by this dance-like and light rhythm. Duke Ellington was one of the first musicians playing swing. Pay attention to the constant triplets and emphasize beats 2 and 4.

Ensemble:

On the following pages I have assembled multi-instrument rhythms from different cultural backgrounds.

STYLES

Latin Basic

First part (cajon comparsa)

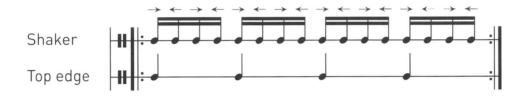

Second part (shaker and cajon)

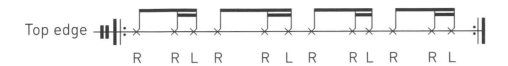

Third part (cajon "La Peru")

STYLES

Like Bossa

First part (shaker)

Shaker

Second part (cajon "La Peru" or cajon comparsa)

Top edge

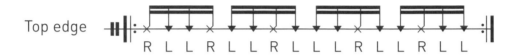

R L L R L L R L L L R L L R L L

Third part

Top edge

Bass

R L L R R L L R R L L R R L L R

STYLES

Samba

First part (cajon comparsa)

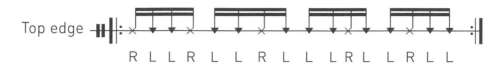

Second part (cajon "La Peru")

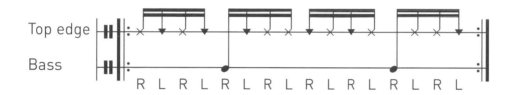

Third part (bass cajon)

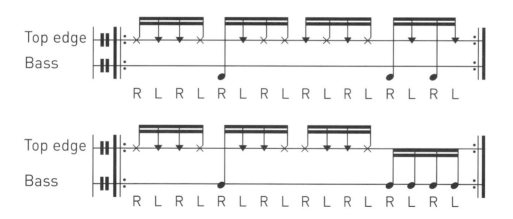

STYLES

Afro Basic

First part (cajon "La Peru")

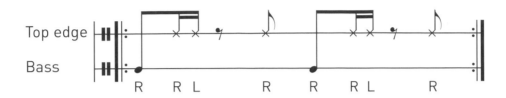

Second part (cajon "La Peru")

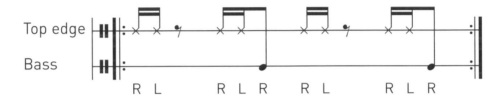

Third part (bass cajon)

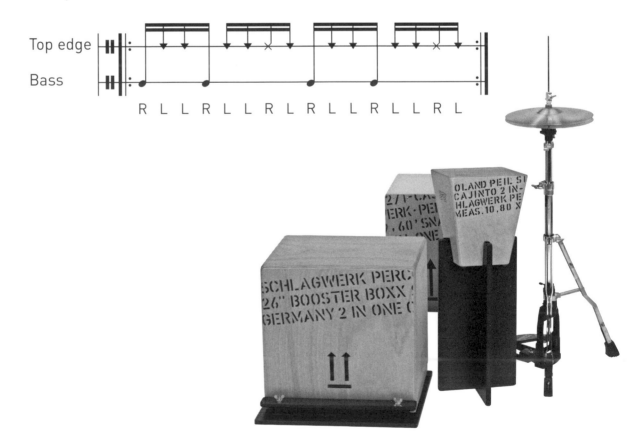

STYLES

Kassa

First part (cajon comparsa)

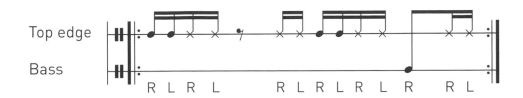

Second part (cajon "La Peru")

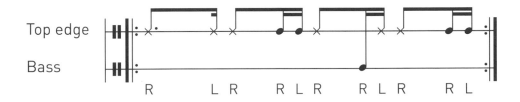

Third part

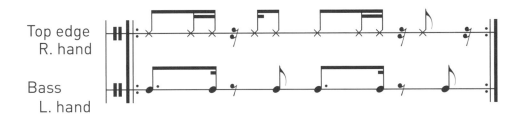

STYLES

Kakilambe

First part (cajon comparsa)

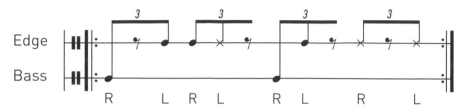

Second part

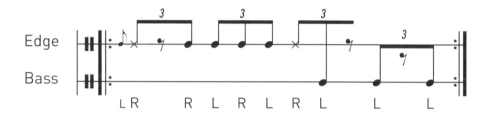

Third part (bass cajon)

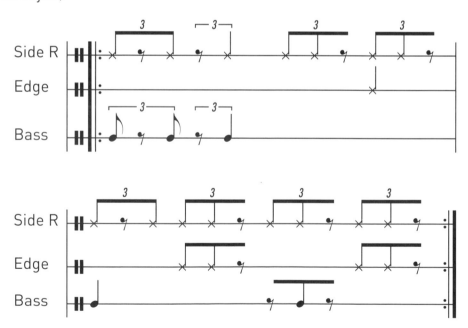

STYLES

Oriental Basic

First part (cajon comparsa)

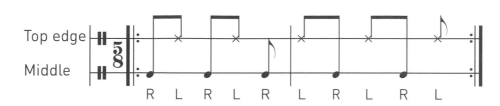

Second part (cajon "La Peru")

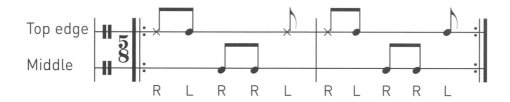

Third part (bass cajon)

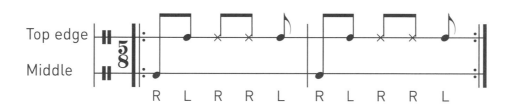

STYLES

Devri Hindi

First part (cajon comparsa)

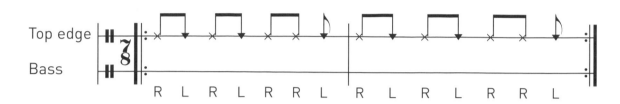

Second part (cajon "La Peru")

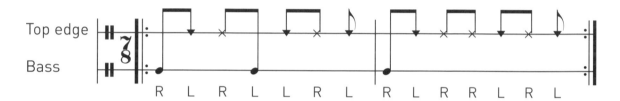

Third part (bass cajon)

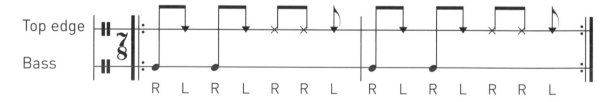

STYLES

Aksak

First part (cajon comparsa)

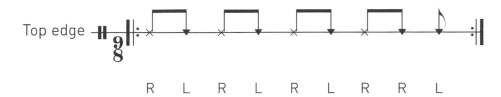

Second part (cajon "La Peru")

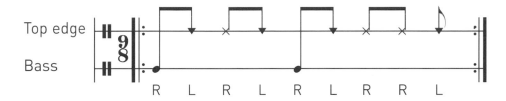

Third part (bass cajon)

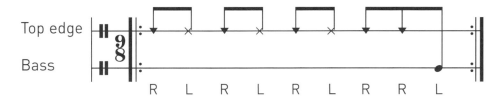

STYLES

Havanna Moon

First part (cajon comparsa)

Second part (cajon "La Peru")

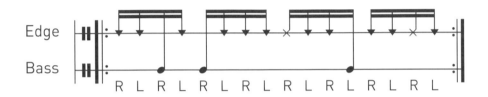

Third part (bass cajon)

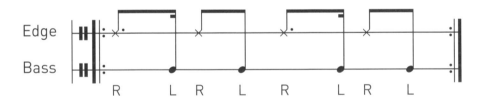

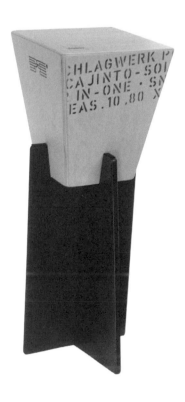

Thanks

This book is dedicated to my girlfriend Silke Al-Taie.

I would like to thank:
- my brother Peter Philipzen (www.Peter-Philipzen.de) for the wonderful compositions.

- Ralf and Jörg Schiemann (www.Schiamo.com) for their patient and precise work during the recording.

- Gerhard and Marianne Priel (www.schlagwerk.com) for their incomparable instruments.

- Jörg Kohlmorgen for the world's best cymbals (www.paiste.com)

- Reiner Hartfil and Stefan Graf (Audio Pro) for the fantastic AKG mics (www.AKG.com)

- Paul Agner for your one-of-a-kind sticks (www.agner-sticks.com)

- Nikolaus Veser for his endurance and the beautiful layout of this book.

See you later ...

Dieter Kropp's
Blues Harp Songbook

Whether you're a beginner or an intermediate player, this book provides you with all you need to know about blues harp playing, from the fundamental basics to such topics as tone shaping, phrasing, articulation and harp equipment. Clearly arranged songs and transparent playalongs help to create an understanding and a feel for the musical form of the blues.

Even if you don't know anything about notation, you will learn all the basic playing techniques. Cool licks and scales help you to expand your playing technique and can be practised immediately with the playalongs of the included CD. Carefully selected songs demonstrate the traditional playing styles of blues. Additional personal tips, explanations and exercises for the single tunes ensure a fast learning progress.

136 pages, CD included!
Format: DIN A4 /8.3" x 11.7"
ISBN: 978-3-8024-0621-8

Voggenreiter

Bessler/Opgenoorth
Keyboard Guide

This practical overview of chords, keys and harmonic relationships has been especially designed with the Jazz, Rock and Pop keyboarder in mind.
It features a new structure that makes it useful for beginners as well as advanced musicians.
This enables you to improve your musical understanding.

104 pages
Format: DIN A5 / 5.8" x 8.3"
ISBN: 978-3-8024-0340-8

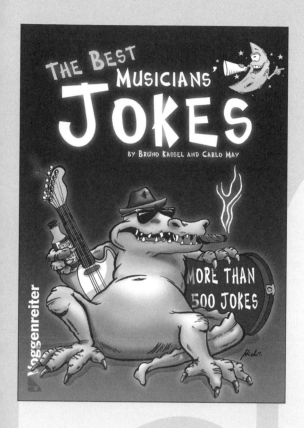

Carlo May/Bruno Kassel
The Best Musicians' Jokes

More than 500 jokes about all musician's genres, plus a foreword written by the famous drummer Pete York.
Carlo May and Bruno Kassel both live in Cologne, Germany and have been musicians since their early teens. Frightened by the perspective of becoming rich and famous, they opted for less dangerous professions. Carlo - a guitar player - was fed up with having his IQ compared to the number of strings on his instrument. He is now a journalist, working for German National Radio (Deutschlandfunk). Bruno - a drummer - used his collection of broken lightbulbs to build his own darkroom. He is now a photographer and music journalist, working for various music magazines.

174 pages
Format: DIN A6 / 4.1" x 5.9" (pocket size!)
ISBN: 978-3-8024-0368-2

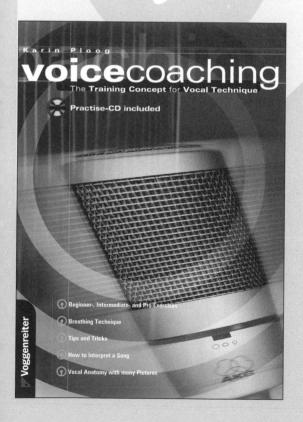

Karin Ploog
Voicecoaching

Here you'll find everything you need to know about developing your voice and a perfect breathing technique. All the exercises are divided into beginner, intermediate und pro level so you can study according to your own level of abilities. This book will support you when having problems with your voice, get you working on interpretation techniques and deepen your musical understanding in general.
Furthermore, you'll get lots of tips and tricks, starting with warming up and continuing up to working in the recording studio. The author – renowned singer, university teacher and studio-voicecoacher – shows you the techniques and tricks of the pros in a clear and easy-to-understand way, complemented with lots of graphics and anatomical drawings. Whether you're self-taught, a music student, or just using this book along with your regular studies – Voicecoaching will be a competent companion for every musical level.

116 pages, CD included!
Format: DIN A4 / 8.3" x 11.7"
ISBN: 978-3-8024-0477-1

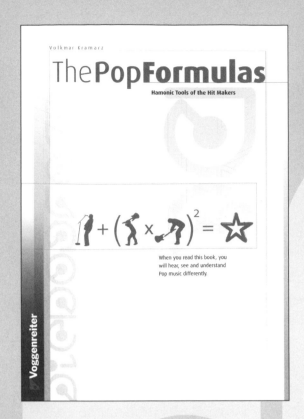

Volkmar Kramarz
The Pop Formulas

Pop and Rock – This is how the stars write their hits!

This book rocks because it teaches Pop and Rock harmonies exclusively and in detail, but in an easy-to-understand and clear manner. Priority is to explain the actual song framework including chords and song structure. This book shows in particular how Rock and Pop become alive – and how this can be achieved.
Reduced to the essentials but entering the subject on a deeper level than any other publication before, this book will definitely change the way Pop and Rock is viewed. After reading this book, you will write differ-ent songs than before – and these may become hits!

160 pages, CD included!
Format: DIN A4 /8.3" x 11.7"
ISBN: 978-3-8024-0620-1

Bessler/Opgenoorth
Elementary Music Theory

The most important basics of music theory explained in an easily understandable way. Some of the topics include: how to read music, intervals, scales, and how the most commonly used instruments create sound. If you always wanted to deepen your under-standing of music theory, but somehow never quite got around to it, this is the book to read.

120 pages
Format: DIN A5 / 5-3/4" x 8-1/4"
ISBN 978-3-8024-0416-0